D0078102

STUDIO TELEVISION PRODUCTION AND DIRECTING

This updated third edition of *Studio Television Production and Directing* introduces readers to the fundamentals of studio and control room production.

Accessible and focused, readers of this updated third edition will learn about essential studio and control room terminology and the common technology package. The text is a back-to-the-basics guide—including principles of directing, assistant directing, technical directing, playback, audio ops, basic studio lighting, an introduction to set design, camera ops, floor directing, story types (VO, VO/SOT, PKG), basic engineering, and more.

Whether an established professional or a student, the book provides readers with the technical expertise to successfully coordinate live or recorded multicamera production.

In this new edition, author Andrew Hicks Utterback offers an expanded glossary and new material on visualization walls, alternative camera mounts, basic engineering, and news narrative diagramming.

Andrew Hicks Utterback, Ph.D. is a Professor in the Department of Communication at Eastern Connecticut State University. As a former Senior Production Technician, he writes from professional experience that includes program credits in master control, as grip, gaffer, A1, camera operator, playback, floor director, technical director, assistant director, and director. As a Professor in the field for 24 years, Dr. Utterback presents the fundamentals of studio television production and directing in a simple and straightforward manner that is clear and unintimidating.

STUDIO TELEVISION PRODUCTION AND DIRECTING

Concepts, Equipment, and Procedures

THIRD EDITION

Andrew Hicks Utterback

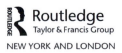
Routledge
Taylor & Francis Group

NEW YORK AND LONDON

Cover image: Courtesy Grass Valley

Third edition published 2023
by Routledge
605 Third Avenue, New York, NY 10158

and by Routledge
4 Park Square, Milton Park, Abingdon, Oxon, OX14 4RN

Routledge is an imprint of the Taylor & Francis Group, an informa business

© 2023 Andrew Hicks Utterback

The right of Andrew Hicks Utterback to be identified as author of this work has been asserted in accordance with sections 77 and 78 of the Copyright, Designs and Patents Act 1988.

All rights reserved. No part of this book may be reprinted or reproduced or utilised in any form or by any electronic, mechanical, or other means, now known or hereafter invented, including photocopying and recording, or in any information storage or retrieval system, without permission in writing from the publishers.

Trademark notice: Product or corporate names may be trademarks or registered trademarks and are used only for identification and explanation without intent to infringe.

First edition published by Routledge 2007
Second edition published by Routledge 2015

ISBN: 978-0-367-19921-0 (hbk)
ISBN: 978-0-367-19922-7 (pbk)
ISBN: 978-0-429-24410-0 (ebk)

DOI: 10.4324/9780429244100

Typeset in Palatino
by SPi Technologies India Pvt Ltd (Straive)

First Edition

For Elias, Anna, and Myles, Susanna,
and Mom and Dad

Second Edition

For all of my students - former, current, future
In Memory of Mom
In Memory of Wayne M. Nesbitt
In Memory of Brian M. Barnard

Third Edition

In Memory of Roger A. Hicks, KCWC-TV,
Lander/Riverton, Wyoming

Dedicated to ALL OF THE PRODUCTION TEAMS AROUND
THE WORLD that made it happen during the
pandemic. Wow … just wow. Thank YOU!

CONTENTS

ACKNOWLEDGMENTS

Writing takes time and attention away from people close to the author. I know that, in one way or another, I owe that time back to my family. THANKS TO ELIAS, ANNA, and MYLES. I'd also like to thank my wife Susanna for tolerating (in good form) my hours and hours (and hours) away from all the things that (still) need doing (insert sigh).

A great deal of what I know about studio television production and directing I learned from Wayne M. Nesbitt.

My Uncle – Roger A. Hicks – deserves recognition for answering many of my television questions over the years and for helping to bring PBS to the State of Wyoming at KCWC, Lander-Riverton. He was a true believer …

Colleagues from Northern Arizona University and Eastern Connecticut State University all contribute to the pedagogy of the manuscript in one way or another. I would like to thank Norm Medoff, Dale Hoskins, Brian Snow, Paul Neuman, and Phil Stewart from NAU.

Jaime Gomez, Denise Matthews, Paul Melmer, Andy Lawrence, Steve Kesten, Lisa Houghtaling, Alex Boyer, and Nick Messina deserve a great deal of credit for tolerating my presence in the ECSU studio over the last 20 years.

I would like to thank ALL of my former students, near and far. A special recognition to all of the NewsWatch44, News22, ETV-News, and ETV-Sports alumni.

Daniel Kershaw and Gennifer Eccles are my patient and tolerant guides at Focal Press/the Taylor & Francis Group.

Manuscript review was patiently handled by William Murphy at Northwest Missouri State University (KNWT-TV) and Dr. Michael Grabowski at Manhattan College.

I WOULD LIKE TO THANK ALL OF THE FOLLOWING PEOPLE FOR ASSISTING ME SO GENEROUSLY WITH THE IMAGE PACKAGE.

Rob Katko at NBCUniversal MSNBC; ESPN Images; Tobin Neis at Barbizon; Wendy Orfan at ETC; Mike Finn at Chauvet; Jay Gravina, Elpi

Klapa, and Valerie Banville at Grass Valley; Guy Low at Electro-Voice and RTS Telex; Megan Bruce at RTS Telex; Alan Venitosh at TELEFUNKEN Elektroakustik; Robert Cook at Videndum Production Solutions; Glenn Anderson at Z Space Creative, Steven Bilow at Telestream; Jonathan Baty at ProAM USA; Megan Solensky at Erie News Now; Tyler Madden at WTOV-9; David Wurtzel at CPTV; Jeffry Langan at CBS2 WBBM-TV Chicago; Gina Bullard at KCTV-5 Kansas City; and Megan Saunders at NBC10 Boston.

I owe the initial momentum of the project to Norman Medoff at Northern Arizona University.

OVERVIEW OF EQUIPMENT AND POSITIONS

The Studio and the Control Room

INTRODUCTION

Studio-based television production is not rocket science. To understand the process of studio production is, to a large extent, a task of learning a new vocabulary, and to a lesser extent, a task of learning how to operate the machines of television production.

Technical proficiency is gained in any television production environment through practice, rehearsal, and repetition. The only path to true fluency in any crew position is the practical performance of studio television work in a professional environment. And, although a great deal of knowledge awaits the television student "on the job," much can be mastered prior to that first production position or internship.

The content that is provided here is limited to the most common jobs associated with the studio and the **control room**. Depending on the size of the television operation, the number of production personnel and their specific job duties will vary widely. For example, in small market stations, the **Director** not only uses the command **cue** language to "call" or "cue" the show, but also operates the video switcher and may be responsible for operating a graphics system as well.

A great deal of geographic (and program genre) variation exists in any given studio production protocol. The "way it is done" in Baltimore will likely differ from the "way it is done" in Salt Lake City. The equipment complement in a given installation will also make necessary variations in protocol. What follows is a lowest common denominator approach – it is not and does not claim to be exhaustive. Variations (when known) may be indicated in the text and will be included in the glossary.

The running example of the book is the affiliate-level live television newscast. Not only is the live newscast a common form of studio production, it is a complex one. It is hoped that mastering a news protocol will

DOI: 10.4324/9780429244100-1

permit the student of television production to work within other genres with relative ease. Almost all of what follows applies to any studio-based television program – live or pre-recorded.

The section that follows provides an overview of the jobs associated with studio-based television production. And, for each crew position, the equipment related to each job will be described.

THE TELEVISION PRODUCTION ENVIRONMENT

The production environment for the typical **network affiliate** newscast can be best understood by dividing the television workspace as follows: the studio; the control room; post-production; and master control.

The Studio and Control Room

The **studio** is the large space where the set for a television program is located. For a live news program, the **anchors** deliver the newscast from an anchor desk (or other type of set) to the viewers. Although it is unusual, some larger studios contain more than one set (for entirely different programs). Commonly, the studio will contain smaller sub-sets that are used in conjunction with the newscast (such as a weather center/desk, traffic news space, or a dedicated interview set).

The **control room** is usually nearby. Often the control room is attached to the studio by a common wall (with or without windows). However, it is not uncommon for the control room to be located away from the studio by some distance (even on a separate floor of a large building). The control room controls the operations of the studio. While control rooms are usually dedicated to a particular studio, it is important to note that some control rooms can control more than one studio.

Post-Production and Master Control

Post-production refers to a space in the television station where video editing activities are conducted. In some stations, traditional editing suites (small rooms) are available and contain the equipment necessary for creating pre-recorded material that can be used in the newscast. As almost all stations have moved to **video file servers** (server-based systems), video editing can occur just about anywhere within the station or in the field where server access is feasible.

Master control refers to the transmission control of the television station itself. Incoming and outgoing microwave and satellite signals are received/transmitted in this area and the final output **mix** of the station

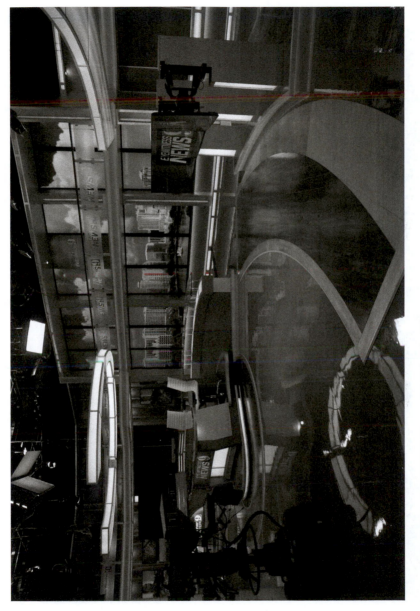

Figure 1.1 Studio with a News Set; WFTV Channel 9 Orlando, FL
(Courtesy Glenn Anderson, Z Space Creative)

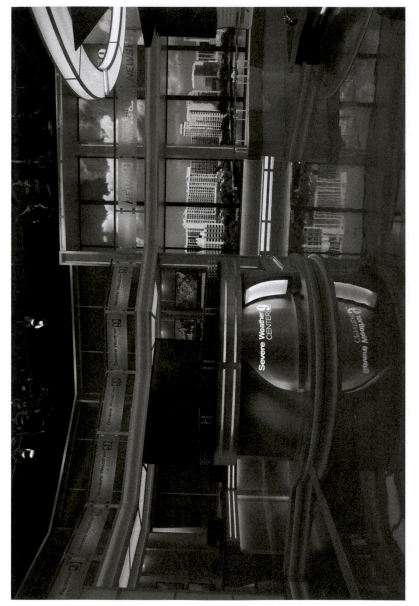

Figure 1.1a Severe Weather Sub-Set; WFTV Channel 9 Orlando, FL
(Courtesy Glenn Anderson, Z Space Creative)

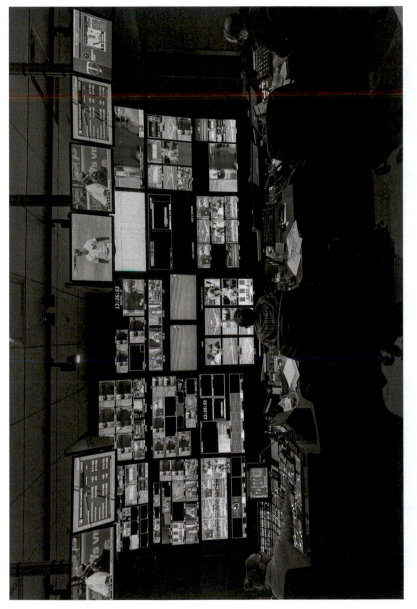

Figure 1.2 Control Room, ESPN Digital Center 2, Bristol, CT – April 1, 2021 – MLB Opening Day.
(Photo by Kelly Backus/Courtesy ESPN Images)

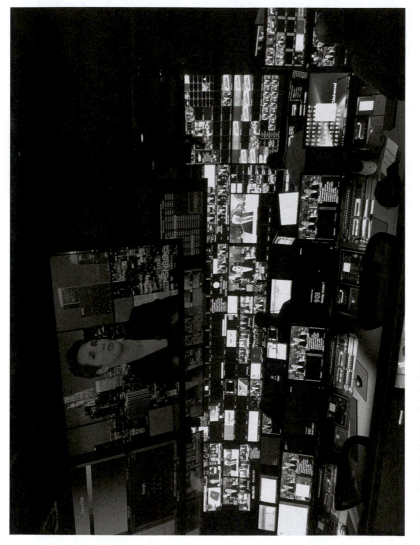

Figure 1.2a Control Room, MSNBC, New York, NY
(Courtesy Rob Katko, MSNBC)

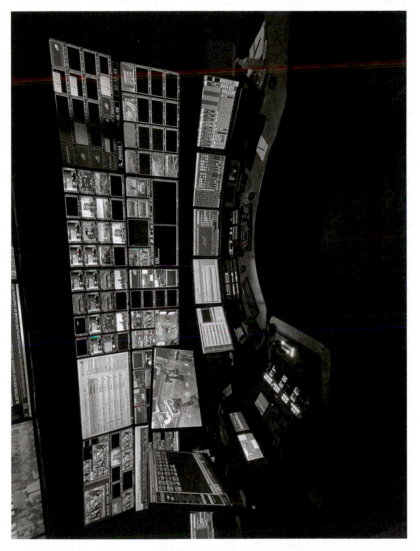

Figure 1.2b Control Room, WBTS – NBC Channel 10 Boston, MA
(Courtesy Megan Saunders, NBC Universal)

is controlled here. Pre-recorded programs, advertising, promotions, and other mastered (finished) video assets are managed from the master control area. Smaller television stations (that are typically a part of an ownership group) may not have their own master control. If this is the case, the stations are likely "hubbed." Hubbed stations are controlled from a "grouped" master control – controlling the outputs of several stations – and can thus share various signal processing and transmission equipment.

THE STUDIO I

The Physical Space

The studio is designed to control light and sound. The physical space is constructed toward this purpose – to some degree – and all studios will share some of the following characteristics. The studio floor is flat and clean so that the **cameras** can move smoothly around the set. The production staff needs to help to keep the floor clean and clear by avoiding practices that create hazards for the cameras (such as leaving unused tape spikes on the floor).

The walls of the studio can be constructed of many types of material (cinderblock, brick, concrete, etc.). If the walls of your studio are covered in stretched fabric, you need to take special care not to touch, puncture, or tear the fabric membrane as it is designed to absorb sound and eliminate echo. Other types of acoustic treatments are also commonly found fastened to the walls of the studio. Ideally, studios are constructed in a fashion to reduce angles, corners, and other flat vertical surfaces in the attempt to control sound. Thus, an ideal studio (for audio control at least) is shaped like an egg!

A few feet out from the physical wall, large curtains or panels of fabric called **cycloramas** are common in television studios. Cycloramas, sometimes called "cycs" are mounted on tracks, come in many colors and most studios will have two or more that surround all or most of the studio. **Hard cycs** can also be found in television studio set-ups. Essentially a set piece, a hard cyc is a large curving platform (shaped like 1/4 of a bowl or a skateboarding quarter-pipe). Hard cycs are used, primarily, when utilizing software-generated, **"virtual" sets**.

The ceiling of the studio is high in order to accommodate physical set materials and the studio lighting system. The studio ceiling may be painted flat black in order to prevent light reflection. Additionally, the added ceiling height in a studio, historically, allows for the efficient removal of heat (primarily generated by traditional, older halogen lighting systems).

The most prominent feature near the ceiling is the **lighting grid**. The lighting grid is made up of pipes called **battens** and the **lighting instruments** hang from these using large c-clamp mounts. A professional lighting grid will be made up of battens running nearly wall to wall, in both directions, approximately 3 feet apart.

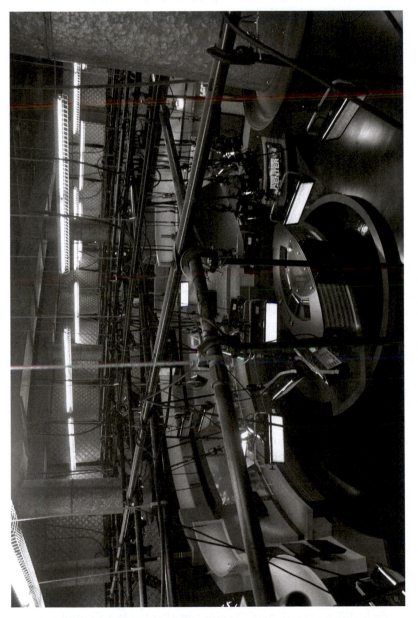

Figure 1.3 Lighting Grid/WSOC Channel 9 Charlotte, NC (Cox Media Group)
(Courtesy Barbizon Lighting Company)

Another item that will either be located in the studio or in the control room is the **lighting board** or console. The lighting board is a computerized "on/off switch" for each lighting instrument. Each instrument can be independently addressed, "tied" to other instruments, and all of the instruments can be controlled at once using the lighting board. Multiparameter lights can be programmed for color and/or movement. Each circuit that is controlled by the lighting board can be fed power incrementally – from 0 to 100 percent. Each modern lighting instrument is also a "computer" with a network address. A lighting network such as this is controlled using the DMX (digital multiplex) protocol. The crew members that are responsible for hanging and aiming the lights are called **Gaffers**. In many professional environments, Gaffers are certified electricians.

Studio Television Cameras

The typical studio will be equipped with three **studio television cameras**. Although many studios have more than three cameras, it would be unusual to find fewer in a typical news set-up. Studio television cameras are non-format specific. The video signal that is generated by the camera can usually be recorded to a variety of **video file formats** (.mov, .wmv, .mp4, etc.). The video signal can typically be acquired in different image shapes or **aspect ratios** (4:3 or 16:9, etc.). The video signal that is generated can be acquired using one of two different **scan protocols** (progressive or interlace). And, the video signal that is generated can usually be acquired utilizing different line **resolutions** (480 **SDTV**, 720 **HDTV**, 1080 HDTV, 2160 4K **UHDTV**, 4320 8K UHDTV, 8640 16K QUHDTV or "Quad").

Historically, studio cameras did not feature on-board recording capability (camcorders always did and still do). Today, the advent and proliferation of **flash memory** technology in the camera industry has reversed the situation. Many studio cameras have on-board recording capability; and, the on-board recording format is almost always a type of flash memory. While the output of the switcher is, ultimately, what represents the program video (what viewers at home will view or what will be recorded), on-board recording permits in-camera ISO (isolation) recording as well.

> *Note*: On-board **ISO recording** is valuable for programs that are prerecorded or produced in an "**as-live**" environment. ISO recordings from each camera allow editors to cover problems in the program video or create entirely different versions of the program after-the-fact. Control room-based ISO recordings can be used in similar fashion or can be used for instant replay, slow motion, etc.

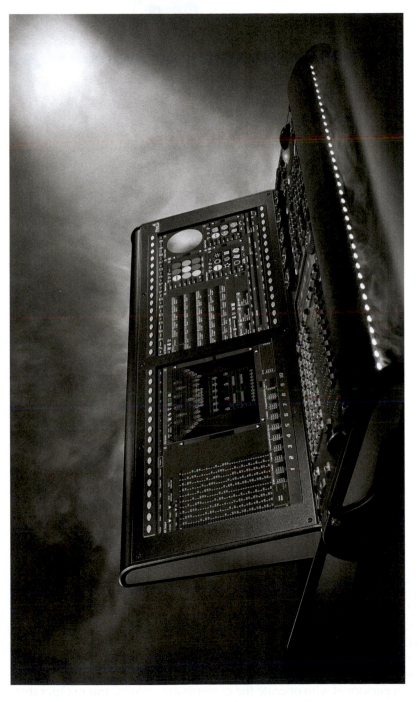

Figure 1.4 Automated Lighting Control Board – Hog4

(Courtesy Electronic Theatre Controls (ETC) and Barbizon Lighting Company)

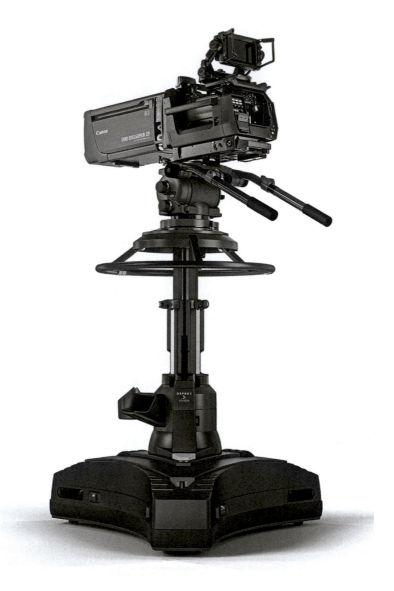

Figure 1.5 Studio Camera Unit

(Courtesy Videndum Production Solutions, Inc.)

All modern studios will be equipped with (at least) high definition cameras (720 or 1080 HDTV) and a few may have ultra high definition cameras **(UHDTV – 4K or 8K)**. While still new, quad ultra high definition cameras are on the horizon **(QUHDTV 16K)**. All modern cameras are digital.

The cameras will be numbered, camera one, two, and three. The production personnel who operate the cameras are called **Camera Operators**; and, the operators will be referred to by the number of the camera they are assigned to. For instance, you might hear, "Hey Camera Two, would you help me move the audio snake?" A number of studios have robotic cameras that can be controlled by joystick and/or computer program – camera control systems or CCS. In the case of robotic cameras, only one production crew member is needed to "drive" (operate) the cameras. The robotic camera control system is typically located in the control room. An alternative is to locate the robotic camera control system in the studio.

THE STUDIO II

The News Set

The primary set for the typical television news program is often centered upon a desk where the anchors sit to deliver the program content. The desk is designed to accommodate four anchors at a time (two news anchors, sports, and weather), although all four are rarely seated at the same time.

In most studios, the desk is part of a permanent set that may include **risers** (a platform to raise the height of the desk) and **flats** (vertical panels that provide a background or "flat wall" to the rear and sides of the desk). One type of flat wall that is fairly common is called a **duratran or translite**. A duratran is a large image printed upon transparent material (plexiglass) and backlit. However, the types of materials that might be utilized to constitute flat walls are too numerous to list here. However, a common (and less expensive) alternative to the duratran is the use of large, independently "fed" studio video monitors (larger LCD panels), video projection, or video walls.

Set materials and props are typically stored inside of an adjacent or attached room called the **scene dock**. A scene dock is simply a storage room that is connected to the studio and is also accessible from the exterior of the building. Large set materials can be off-loaded and brought through the scene dock into the studio.

Multiple **video monitors** will be positioned throughout the studio as well. The monitors allow for studio personnel (including the talent) to see different video feeds routed from the control room. The production crew member responsible for studio set-up and assembling the set is called a **Grip**.

Since most news operations use a permanent news set, Grips are not needed on a frequent basis for a full, daily set-up. Commonly, stations will contract set-design firms to design, build, and install the news set. Grips are commonly tasked during production with other jobs (handling boom-mounted mics, operating jib crane-mounted cameras, cable management, etc.).

Traditionally, the weather forecast is delivered from a spot in front of a green screen or chroma key colored cyclorama (or **chroma key wall**) located near the primary set. The unusual, and highly saturated color of the background permits the weather anchor's camera image to be keyed

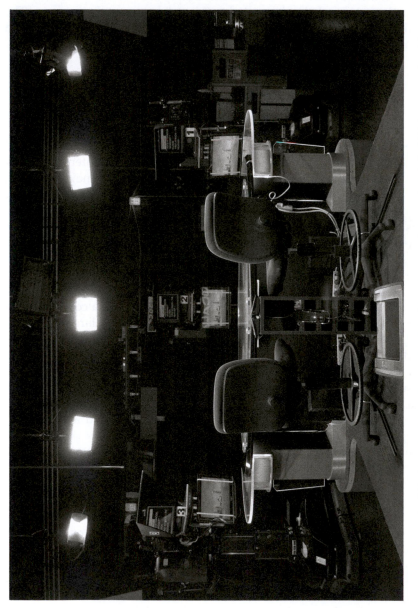

Figure 1.6 News Set from a reverse angle/WKMG Channel 6 Orlando, FL (Graham Media Group); note: Bank Lighting (Courtesy Barbizon Lighting Company)

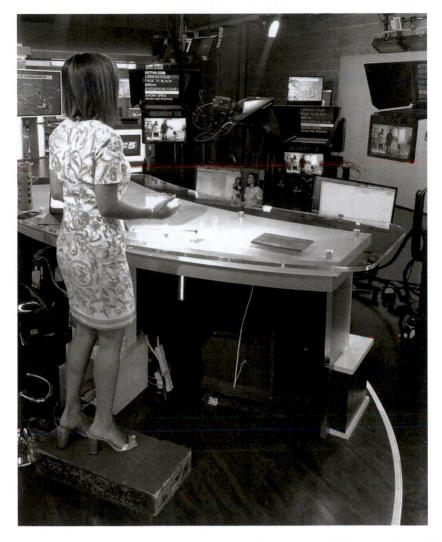

Figure 1.6a News Set from a reverse angle/ KCTV Channel 5 Kansas City, MO
(Gray Television)

(Courtesy Gina Bullard)

over (layered over) the weather graphics. It is in this manner that the weather anchor appears to "float" in the foreground, over the weather graphics. Alternatively, the weather forecast may be delivered from a location in front of a large monitor, video wall, or other type of video projection screen. In this case, the weather anchor is simply standing in front of a monitor or screen that is displaying (being "fed") the weather graphics. Often, a separate smaller set area is located in the studio and is dedicated to weather news (a weather desk or "weather center").

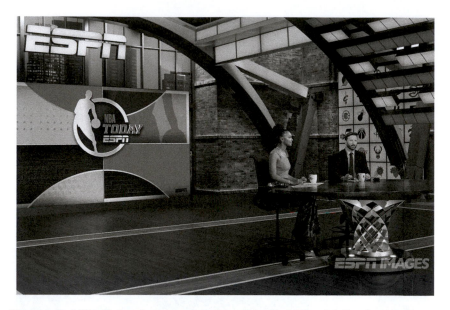

Figure 1.6b NBA Today, Los Angeles, CA – July 19, 2022 – LA Production Center
note: duratran or translite type of "flat wall"

(Photo by Kelly Backus/courtesy ESPN Images)

Sports news is most commonly delivered from one of two locations. First, the sports anchor may simply join the news anchors at the primary news desk. Second, the sports anchor may be located in the studio at a sub-set specifically created for sports (a sports desk or other dedicated location). Other variations for delivery of sports news are routinely in practice, including set-ups similar to weather.

As a matter of course, other types of dedicated news content may be handled in similar fashion. Examples include: Editorials, Traffic News, Political News, Consumer News, Health News, etc.

Patch Panels and Signal Routing

Located on the wall of the studio – often in many locations – are hook-up jacks for audio, video, clock, intercom, and other signals that pass between the studio and the control room. These hook-up jacks are located together and are called **patch panels**.

Prior to the show, the person responsible for audio in the control room (**Audio or A1**) or a dedicated "studio" audio crew member (**A2**) will connect audio cables to route the audio signals from the **microphones** to a patch panel (and therefore on to the control room). In some studios, the audio is routed to the patch panel through an **audio snake** that permits multiple mic hook-ups. Another common variation is to use wireless

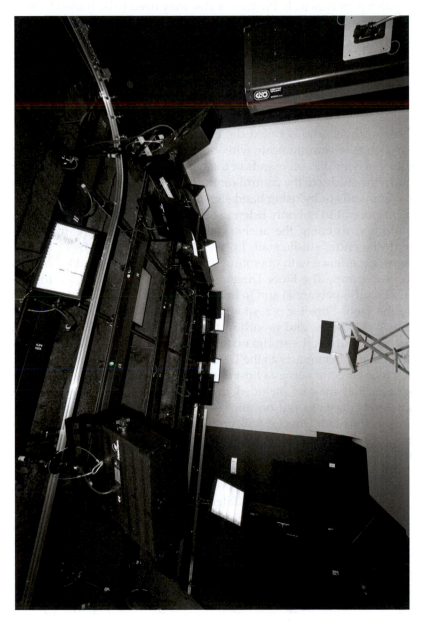

Figure 1.7 Chroma key hard cyc
(Courtesy Barbizon Lighting Company)

microphones. In this case, the audio operator(s) will need to system check the wireless transmitters and receivers during pre-production.

Other members of the production crew may need to make connections to the patch panels as well. Program video may need to be routed to monitors, intercom connections may need to be made, and even cameras can (in some studios) be hooked into different panels.

THE STUDIO III

Floor Director

The boss of the studio is called the **Floor Director**. The Floor Director's primary job is to communicate with, or cue, the news anchors. The Floor Director can hear the commands of the Director using an intercom system that links the studio to the control room. The Floor Director will cue using voice commands or by using hand signals (when a microphone is active), so it is important to not only listen to but to watch the Floor Director.

In addition to cuing the anchors, the Floor Director is communicating with the entire studio staff. In the ideal situation, the Floor Director has some experience with operating cameras, lighting, set assembly, and audio procedures. The Floor Director is frequently called upon to assist the other studio personnel and to help troubleshoot equipment problems. Often, the Floor Director is responsible for studio safety as well. As the Director's eyes, ears, and mouth in the studio, the Floor Director is the ultimate authority in the studio once the program begins. It is in this way that the Floor Director acts as the Director's representative in the studio.

The Floor Director acts as a host in the studio for the news anchors and any guests that may be included in the program. Floor Directors help anchors and guests to put on microphones and "dress" the mic cables. And, while the Floor Director will, on occasion, "talk back" to the Director, it is poor form for any of the production staff to use the intercom system to chat.

Talent

Finally, the **talent** of the news program, the anchors, work in the studio during the live-portion of the program. Typically, the anchors will be seated and put on microphones on the set 10 minutes or so before the program begins – **mic checks** will be conducted (along with other technical checks). Often the anchors will spend the last few minutes before the show goes live reviewing, marking, and editing a hard (paper) copy of the script.

The Floor Director will review any unusual events for the program that follows with the anchors and the rest of the studio crew as necessary (guest interviews, special camera moves). In the common network affiliate newscast, the talent consists of two news anchors (one who is often "senior" in status), a weather anchor, and a sports anchor.

THE CONTROL ROOM

Equipment and Crew Positions

The control room "controls" the studio. While a wide array of audio- and video-processing gear will be installed in the control room, and, all control rooms will differ to some extent, most will include the following: a **monitor wall** or **multi-viewer**, an **audio console**, a **video switcher**, a **teleprompting computer**, one or more **graphics computers**, an **engineering** space, and a section for recording the show and controlling **playback** of pre-recorded video. Depending on the installation, a **lighting board** or console may be positioned inside of or nearby to the control room.

Monitor Wall or Multi-Viewer

The monitor wall or multi-viewer is centered around two larger video monitors that display **Preview (PVW)** video (positioned left) and **Program (PGM)** video (typically positioned right). The Program video monitor displays the video source that is "active, live, on-line," or "the video signal that is being recorded or viewed at home." The Preview monitor shows the video source that is next or "on-deck" for Program. Note: preview is often called **Preset (PST)**.

Surrounding these two large monitors are smaller video monitors (monitor wall) that display the video sources available for use by the production crew. These smaller monitors will show studio cameras, microwave feeds, satellite feeds, graphics, playback, and other video sources that can be activated or routed to Preview and Program.

A very common variation on the monitor wall is the use of **multi-viewers**. Multi-viewers are very large monitors that can display (as the name suggests) multiple video feeds at the same time. The screen is simply divided or arranged (within the limits of the software) into two larger screens (preview and program) and/or smaller screens (video sources).

The Video Switcher and "Technical Director"

A prominent feature of the control room is the **video switcher**. The video switcher is a video selection device. The switcher controls the video sources that are activated to Preview and Program and is operated by the **Technical Director (TD)**. The final video feed from the video switcher is called **video program**. The video switcher is discussed in detail in a chapter that follows as is another prominent feature of the control room area – the audio board.

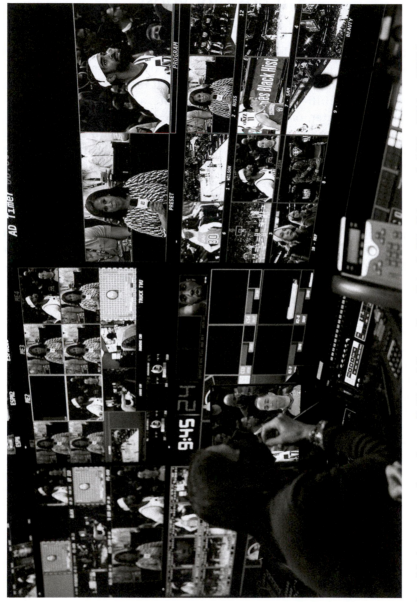

Figure 1.8 A multi-viewer type of monitor wall, Digital Center One – Bristol, CT – February 9, 2022 – NBA on ESPN (Photo by Kelly Backus/courtesy ESPN Images)

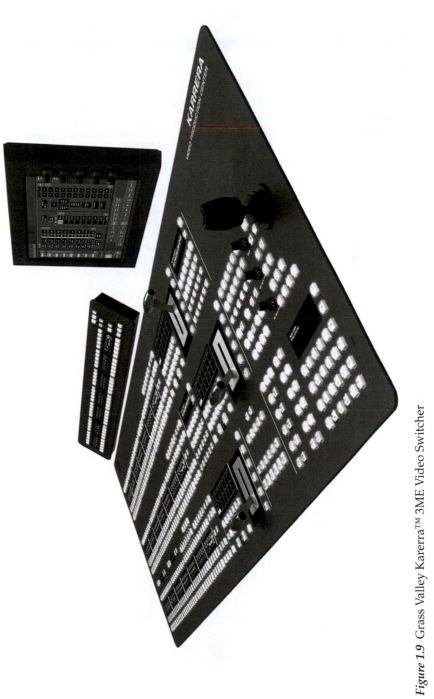

Figure 1.9 Grass Valley Karerra™ 3ME Video Switcher
(Courtesy Grass Valley)

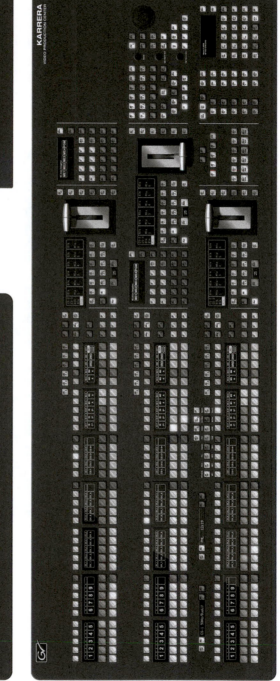

Figure 1.9a Panel Schematic of the Grass Valley Karerra™ 3ME Video Switcher
(Courtesy Grass Valley)

The Audio Board and "Audio"

The **audio board** may be located in the control room proper (with everything else) but it is more common to find it in a smaller adjacent room (**audio booth** or **audio control**). The audio board is an audio selection device that is operated by a crew member called **"Audio"** or identified as the **"A1."** The audio feed from the audio board (the final mix) is called **audio program**. **Audio monitors** – heavy duty speakers – will be located near to the monitor wall to permit the control room crew to listen to audio program.

THE PRODUCTION CREW I

The Graphics Computer and "Graphics"

The graphics computer is operated by a crew member who is commonly called "**graphics**." The graphics computer can create, store, and recall different kinds of graphics: **character generation (CG)**, **still-store (SS)**, **2D** and **3D** graphics, **animations**, maps, and so forth. CG is the creation of alphanumeric text as a video signal. A good example of CG is when the anchor's name is keyed (layered) over a camera image of the anchor or at the end of the program – when the credits are "rolled."

The still-store function centers upon still-image processing. The graphics computer can store high resolution images, capture images from other video sources (a **frame "freeze"**), and access images from subscription image databases (e.g., AP Images). Typically, a graphics computer can edit or modify the image file in almost any imaginable fashion. A graphics computer can combine these images with CG to create entirely new graphics. The process of combining images and text is almost limitless in terms of layering.

A variation of still-store capability is an embedded still image system inside of the video switcher itself (of course, this functionality depends on make/model of the switcher). Thus, it is quite possible that a control room may have more than one still-store in use (one embedded in the switcher, another as a part of the graphics computer).

Animations, quite simply, are graphics that move. A very basic 2D animation might be an image or station logo that slides (flips, dissolves, wipes, etc.) onto the screen. A 3D animation might be a six-sided cube, with a separate image assigned to each surface that simply rotates. The possibilities with animations are truly endless and are limited only by the capabilities of the graphics software used to create them.

It is important to note that many control rooms will separate the CG, still store, and animation functions into three separate computers, workspaces, and crew positions. However, professional grade graphics systems can handle all three functions from a single machine. The more complex

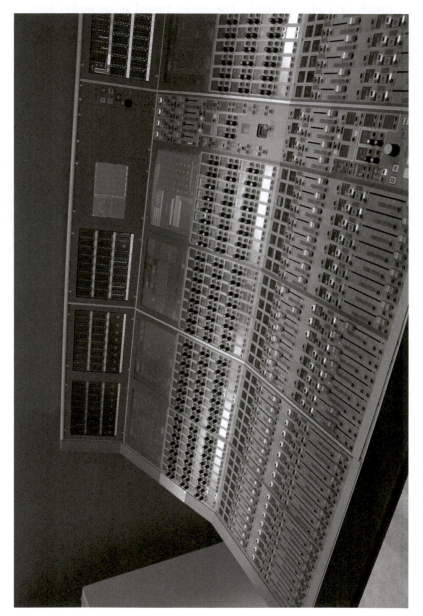

Figure 1.10 Calrec Apollo Audio Board

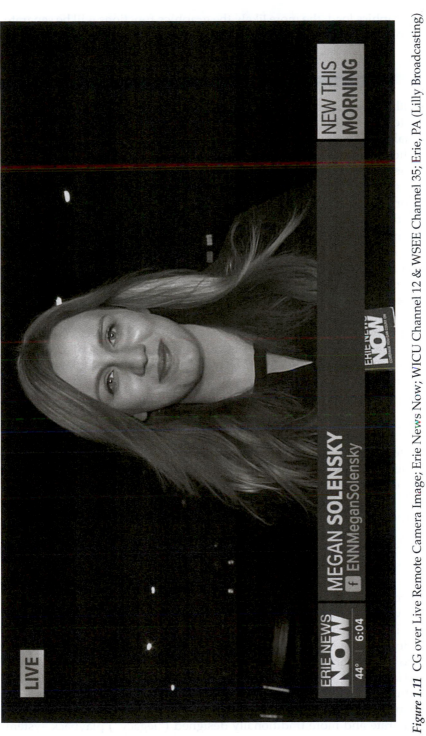

Figure 1.11 CG over Live Remote Camera Image; Erie News Now; WICU Channel 12 & WSEE Channel 35; Erie, PA (Lilly Broadcasting) (Courtesy Megan Solensky)

the graphics load, the more likely the graphics functions will be separated or isolated.

The Prompting Computer and "Prompter"

Another computer in the control room is the **teleprompting computer**. The teleprompter transforms the script for the show into a scrollable video signal that is transmitted to a viewing system mounted on the front of the studio cameras.

The teleprompter controls the word processing and organization of the final script for the program. The collation of all of the stories occurs in the teleprompter; and all final changes to the script are made by the producing staff through this computer system. The person who operates the teleprompting computer is called the "**teleprompter**" or "**prompter**" for short.

In more modern installations, the basic teleprompting computer has been replaced by a machine that is running software that is far far more powerful than basic teleprompting software. **Newsroom Computer Systems (NCS or NRCS)** are **media object server (MOS)** based systems that manage and organize all of the media assets needed for a show (scripts, audio files, video files, graphics files, etc.). The three common versions in use are the AP's ENPS, Avid's Media Central, and Octopus X). At this point, the personal computer PC that was formally known as the teleprompter is really more of a station for the Line Producer.

Playback

The television program is recorded and any pre-recorded material that is needed for the show is controlled from the **playback** position. **Playback** is responsible for operating any number of video recording and **video playback devices**. Historically, pre-recorded material was "rolled" from videotape. Today, it is more common that pre-recorded material is "played" from a video server of some type or **digital disk recorder** (DDR) – even though many folks still say "roll" to activate the **clip**. A good example of this is when a sports anchor is discussing a UCONN Women's basketball game from earlier in the day while the viewer at home is watching the pre-recorded footage of that game (a VO type of clip).

A variation of playback capability is an embedded system inside of the video switcher itself (of course, this functionality depends on make/model of the switcher). Simply put, the Technical Director has the capability to activate or playback pre-recorded material from within the switcher interface.

Thus, it is quite possible that a control room may have more than one capability for playback (one system embedded in the switcher, another as a separate and more traditionally designed ("legacy") playback system).

To add one more layer of complexity to the consideration of playback, consider that many graphics computers can be configured to store and playback video *and* trigger external playback devices and/or video server control devices as well.

It is important to note that in many control rooms playback is located in an adjacent room (as is common with audio). The number and type of playback machines available will vary by facility. For a typical newscast, historically, at least four machines were utilized (one to record, three for playback). Common today is the use of two devices (one to record, one for playback). However, quad and multiple channel servers can both record and playback at the same time (thus, one device "playing back" on three channels and recording on one – or some other combination). Be aware that a common tactic is to "letter" playback devices (A, B, C, etc.), in order to avoid confusion with the "numbered" cameras (Camera One, Camera Two, etc.).

THE PRODUCTION CREW II

The Broadcast Engineer

The task of the **Broadcast Engineer** during a live-production is two-fold. First, all audio and video signal routing is the responsibility of the Engineer. **Live-feeds**, for example, will need to be routed as sources to the control room (usually from master control) on an as-needed basis. Another example is the appropriate routing of video and audio signals both to and from the recording and playback machines. Video, audio, intercom, clock, and other signals will need to be routed between the control room and the studio as well.

Equipment troubleshooting is a common secondary task during routing procedures. Prior to and during the show, the Engineer is responsible for the **Camera Control Units (CCUs)**. Before the show, the Engineer will be sure to white-balance and register the cameras. By using the **waveform monitor** and **vectorscope**, the Engineer can adjust how each camera "sees" individual colors and values (like red, green, blue, black, and white) so that the cameras are "balanced" or matched. During the program, the Engineer (or dedicated staff called "**shaders**" – aka **Video Operators**) can use the CCUs to make adjustments to the iris settings on the camera lens or to "ride gain" – adjust the strength of the video signal level.

Assistant Director (AD)

Live television programs have to begin and end on time. The responsibility of timing a show (both forwards and backwards) belongs to the **Assistant Director (AD)**. The AD will use a Master Clock in order to accomplish

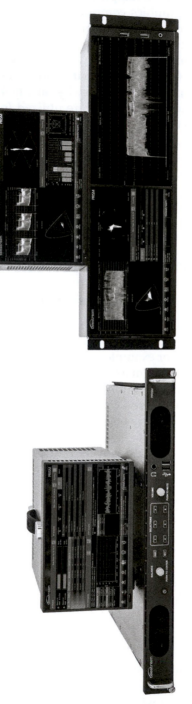

Figure 1.12 Engineering Test Equipment; waveform monitors and vectorscopes
(Courtesy Telestream)

show timing. The clock will either be set to count up from zero or count down from a pre-set show length (like 28:30). In this manner, the AD can announce information such as "we are 10 minutes into the show and we have 18 minutes 30 seconds left."

Another very important job for the AD is the timing of any pre-recorded material used for the show. The AD will need to know the precise length of each pre-recorded video clip to be used in the program. In this way, the AD knows exactly when the clip will end (so a smooth transition can be made back to the studio) and when graphics can be used in conjunction with the clip. In order to accomplish clip timing, an AD will use a stop watch. Often, the stop watch of choice for Assistant Directors is still an old-fashioned analog watch (like the classic 60 Minutes watch) rather than the more common digital stopwatch (more on this in Chapter 8). It is important to remember that the Assistant Director's job is to handle timing, not merely to "assist" the Director as a gopher.

If a station does not use an AD, it is common for the Producer of the newscast to handle timing the show and the Director to take charge of clip and graphics timing.

Another variation on the timing of video clip playback is the use of video servers or DDRs that have embedded "clocks" that can be viewed by the control room staff as the clip plays. While the viewer at home can see a clean feed of video, the production crew is viewing the video with an overlay of a countdown. In yet another wrinkle, some video servers can "trigger" the graphics computer automatically.

DIRECTING AND PRODUCING

Director

Finally, the **Director** is the leader and supervisor of the entire production crew. During the actual program, the Director "cues" or "calls" commands to the production crew using the intercom system. While the Director usually does not operate any particular piece of equipment, the Director does use the script to call audio and video **transitions** for the duration of the program. The Director's cues are called the **command cue language**.

The most effective Directors are very familiar with all of the crew positions and responsibilities as well as much of the production equipment. New Directors find that it is very difficult to lead and supervise that which they do not fully understand. During the program, when the studio is "live," the Director is at the top of the personnel hierarchy. However, a television newscast is a co-creation between the Producer and the Director. The Director is responsible for the technical execution of the program. The Producer is responsible for the content.

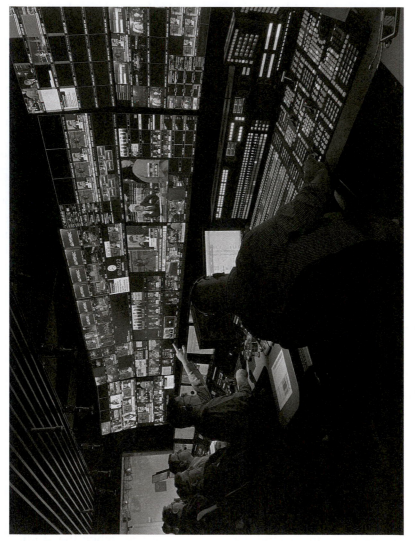

Figure 1.13 Director in the Control Room, MSNBC, New York, NY

(Courtesy Rob Katko, MSNBC)

Producer

The **Producer** is the person responsible for the content of the program – the scripts, the stories, and the pre-recorded video clips. Prior to the broadcast, the Producer works with news, weather, and sports personnel to plan, organize, and construct the newscast.

The Producer will be located in the Control Room during the show. The Producer may make content changes on the fly that the production crew will need to respond to (like adding or cutting material). The Producer may also need to communicate with the anchors during the show using the **Interrupt Foldback (IFB)** system (the little ear piece in the anchor's ear is a tiny headphone and IFB permits the Producer to "cut-in" through audio program (using a microphone in the control room) in order to speak to the anchor).

Producers do "come in many flavors." At times, you may encounter members of the producing staff identified as: Executive Producers, Associate Producers (AP), Assistant Producers, Line Producers, Writers, etc.

AND THE REST ...

The following section describes members of the production staff that may (or may not) be utilized in a particular production operation.

A **Set Designer** is a person who designs sets for particular programs. A set designer is typically a hired contractor or consultant brought in from outside of the television station or network. Similar to designing a house, a set designer will create "blueprints" for a program in consultation with the Producer and Director. Larger stations and networks may employ "in-house" set designers.

A **Lighting Designer or Lighting Director (LD)** is a person who designs the lighting for a particular set. Usually, the LD is working in conjunction with the Set Designer; and, more often than not, both designers are from the same contracting/consulting firm. A lighting designer, working with a more or less completed set design, will overlay a lighting design (or lighting "blueprint") on top of or integrated with the set blueprint. Larger stations and networks may employ "in-house" lighting designers. A Lighting Director may oversee the placement of the lighting instruments and may operate the lighting board.

Media Asset Managers (formerly "tape librarians") are in charge of managing the video, graphic, and audio assets of a particular TV show, TV station, or network. If a producer needs footage of Martin Luther King's "I have a dream" speech, footage of the moon landing, or quite simply a picture of a Calico Cat, Media Asset staff can assist. Additionally, Media Asset personnel are tasked with organizing and archiving current programming and other newly acquired or created assets. Media Asset personnel may be responsible for video editing tasks as well.

Other specialties in the television production business include hair and make-up (and sometimes wardrobe). Prior to each show, the talent and other on-air guests may be subject to the expert ministrations of these production crew members.

2

AUDIO

INTRODUCTION

The production tasks associated with audio control in the studio production environment are the primary responsibility of two important production technicians: the **Audio Operator (A1)** and (if need be) the **Audio Assistant (A2)**. The tasks associated with these positions are detailed in this chapter.

Depending on the design of the control room, the audio control space will be located either in the control room itself or in an isolated booth nearby. The booth style of audio installation is ideal and permits the technician to concentrate on the characteristics of the program audio with greater clarity apart from the distractions of the rest of the control space. The primary job of Audio is to control audio program. **Audio Program** is the final mix of audio that is sent out for transmission or recorded.

AUDIO CONTROLS

The primary responsibility of the technician in charge of audio in a studio production environment is to operate the **audio board** or "console." The job is simply called **Audio (or A1)**, rather than the more formal "audio operator" or some other title. Audio anticipates and responds to commands from the Director, activating and mixing audio sources as needed and on-demand. To understand the job of Audio, one must understand the basics of audio board operation.

DOI: 10.4324/9780429244100-2

The Audio Board

An audio board is an audio selection device. **Audio sources** are devices that acquire or generate audio and are wired as inputs to the board. Common audio sources that Audio can select from include the studio microphones: MIC 1, MIC 2, MIC 3, etc; audio from a dedicated audio player of some type or an audio file-server; audio that is sourced from the various *video* playback devices: digital disk recorders (DDRs), video file-servers (stand-alone or perhaps embedded in the video switcher); audio sourced from a satellite feed; audio sourced from a microwave feed; audio coming in from bonded cellular remotes; and, the audio board itself is an audio source: for example, test **tone** is self-generated by the board. (It is important to remember that one could have any number of microphones, playback devices, satellites, microwaves, and bonded cellular feeds, and other audio sources depending on the size and configuration of the facility).

The Lake of Audio

In order to better understand how an audio board actually works, consider the following conceptual description: for now, go with the idea that the audio board is like a large lake – a lake of audio. Flowing into the lake are many individual streams of audio; and, each stream represents a source of audio (like a microphone). Flowing out of the lake is one river of audio – **Audio**

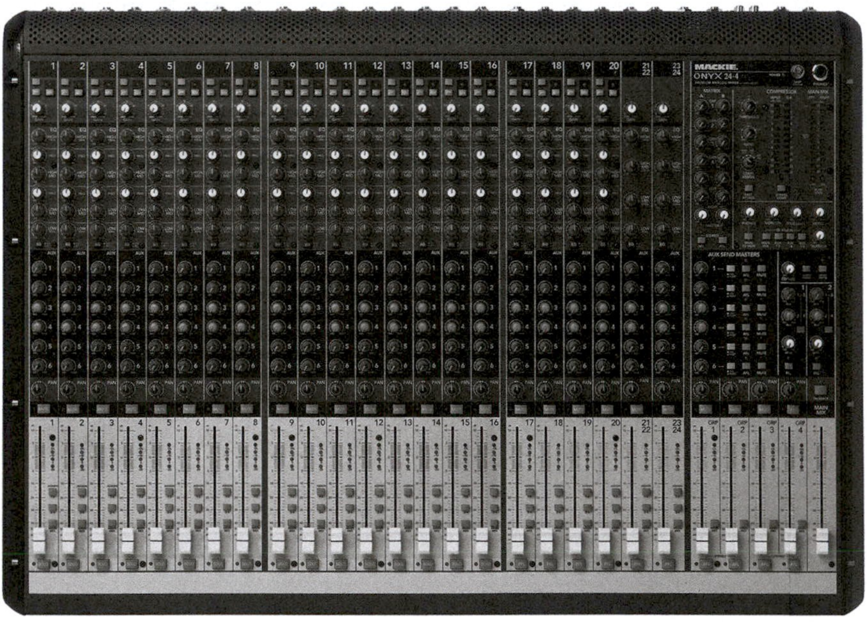

Figure 2.1 Audio Board
(Courtesy Mackie)

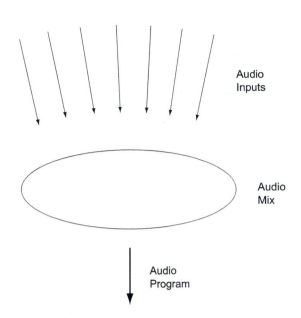

Audio
Inputs

Audio
Mix

Audio
Program

Figure 2.2 The Lake of Audio

Program – and program is the final mix that is sent out, recorded, or eventually heard through the speakers of the television set at home.

AUDIO FLOW

Input and Output Faders

A typical audio board will be built with numbered vertical rows of **input faders** with fader knobs that slide up and down along the bottom of the panel and located closest to the operator. The majority of the **faders** are identical and control audio sources or inputs – and these begin on the absolute left of the board, continue across the middle of the console, and end (usually) at about three quarters or so of the way across.

The faders located from this point onward – the right hand quarter of the console – control special input functions (faders used for "grouping" sources) and special output functions (auxiliary "send" controls for dedicated outputs).

The very last fader on the bank controls the output of the board and is the **Master Fader**. The master fader controls the strength of audio program; and, not uncommonly this fader is a different color than the rest and (again) is the very last one (or less commonly it will be two faders side by side) on the farthest right side of the board.

Note: if you have two faders controlling program, one is for **Channel 1** (Left) and the other is for **Channel 2** (Right).

Mono and Stereo

Audio sources will either be **mono** or **stereo**. For example, microphones are mono sources and audio servers are stereo sources. Mono means that the source is generating and sending one unique, individual, and distinct channel or "line" of audio. Stereo means that the source is generating or has the capacity to generate two unique, individual, and distinct channels or "lines" of audio.

Video playback devices, generally speaking, generate two channels of source audio. However, some generate four channels of source audio and are handled as stereo sources – (4-channel – pairing channel 1 with channel 3 on a fader and channel 2 with channel 4 on a fader).

The Important idea to retain here is that some audio inputs or sources will be controlled with one fader (mono) and others with two (stereo).

Important note: (two channels of source audio) are typically handled with two separate input faders (one for Channel 1 Left; one for Channel 2 Right). However, it is not uncommon to see one input fader controlling a stereo source. A stereo **input fader** uses one physical fader strip to handle both channels. The bummer with the set-up is that the operator has little or no *easy* control of each separate channel. What you do to one channel, you automatically do to the other. In this sense, the channels are "tied" together.

Remember, the Master Fader will either be set up for control as one fader or as two faders located side by side. Audio Program, the output of the console, is typically a stereo (two line) output.

Not to make it more complicated but:

Mono – one unique, individual, distinct line of audio
Stereo – two unique, individual, distinct lines of audio
Quadrafonic – four unique, individual, distinct lines of audio
5.1 Surround Sound – six unique, individual, distinct lines of audio
7.1 Surround Sound – eight unique, individual, distinct lines of audio
Note: various Surround Sound protocols fit in this space (between 7.1 and 22.2) mostly public movie theatre standards (7.1.2; 7.1.4; 10.2; 11.1).

22.2 – and the ridiculous – the UHDTV standard for audio – 24 unique, individual, distinct lines of audio.

Splits and Mixing Down

One point that the beginning student of audio should be aware of is the idea that a mono signal can be "split" to form two channels of duplicate audio (what is coming out of the left speaker is exactly the same as what is coming out of the right speaker). Mono splitting really has no limit. And, a stereo split is similar. The left channel can be split to form two channels and the right channel can be split to form two channels – for a total of four and so on and so on.

Mixing down is where two channels are combined. Thus, using a mixer, a stereo signal (two) can be combined (mixed together) to form a single channel. Again, there really is no limit to this idea – quad mixed down to stereo mixed down to mono is 4 to 2 to 1.

The Audio Flow

Again consider the "lake-of-audio" example. Each input fader (source) is like a dam that controls the flow of audio into the lake. When the fader is "up," the audio is flowing in. When the fader is down, the audio flow is stopped. The primary **output fader**, and you should **focus** on the Master Fader at this point, also controls audio flow like a dam. When the Master Fader is up, the audio may flow out of the lake. When the Master Fader is down, the audio is held inside of the lake.

It is possible then, to (1) allow audio to flow in *and* out – through the lake – (both an input fader and the Master Fader are pushed up); (2) to allow audio to flow in *and not* out (an input fader up and the Master Fader pushed down); or (3) to allow no flow at all (all faders down). The amount of audio that flows in, through, and out of the lake is determined then by the position of each little "dam" (fader) in the audio stream. You should be able to imagine, then, how it is possible that two or more *sources* can flow into the lake individually, be combined together and "mix" in the lake, and then flow out in the final river of audio program (the final mix). The flow of the audio is measured in terms of signal strength.

SIGNAL STRENGTH

Volume and **signal strength** are two separate concepts from the same family. Volume is a human perception of loudness. Signal strength, on the other hand, is a measurement of how much voltage is associated with an audio signal. The primary concern for the crew member assigned to the Audio position is how strong an audio signal is, not how loud it seems to the ear.

In order to adjust the strength of an audio signal, the voltage of the input streams of audio and the voltage of the output stream (audio program) must be measured. The legacy analog measurement for audio is the **Volume Unit (VU)**. Using a VU measure, a signal flow is ideal at an average peak of about 0 VU.

However, since digital audio processing is the norm, audio technicians most commonly use the **decibel scale (dB)**. What is a decibel? Well, a decibel is one-tenth of a "bel" (B). A bel (B) is named in honor of – you guessed it – Alexander Graham Bell. In essence, a decibel is a unit that is used to measure the relative strength of an audio signal.

dBFS and dBu

dBFS stands for decibel (dB) full scale (FS). dBFS is a measure of the amplitude (the height) of an audio wave – from the bottom curve to the top curve. The meter associated with dBFS starts at the bottom on a negative number (–72dBFS) and ends at the top at zero (0dBFS).

An audio wave that is at or exceeding zero is referred to as "clipped" – the peaks and valleys of the waves are simply cut off (or, if you will, visually flattened). On an audio meter that is marked dBFS, a signal that is full zero or beyond is said to be in "OL" or OverLoad. Another way to understand this is that the electrical audio signal is no longer converted to sound by a speaker, it is simply generating heat.

dBu stands for decibel (dB) unloaded (u). dBu is a measure of voltage rather than wave amplitude. The meters associated with dBu start at the bottom on a negative number (around –60dBu) and ends at the top near positive 20 (+20dBu). Thus, the dBu meter is indicating the "electrical strength" of an audio signal – the voltage.

OK … so what do you need to know to run an audio board?

A digital signal flow is ideal at an average peak of –20dBu.

The primary task for Audio is to monitor and adjust signal flow during the program using each input fader and the Master output fader. Signal flow above the ideal risks **overmodulation**, noise, and distortion (or OverLoad). Signal flow below the ideal is too weak, perhaps imperceptible, and **undermodulated**.

The only way to monitor signal flow is by using the meters located on the audio board itself. Each input fader will have a dedicated, singular meter to measure *incoming flow* (or **pre-fader** signal strength). The Master Fader will typically have a dual meter (two channel) to measure the flow of the **post-fader** output – Audio Program.

AUDIO OPERATIONS

Balancing the Inputs

One of the more common issues associated with operating an audio board is when an audio source is flowing either too high or too low *from the source*. To adjust a high flowing source, the typical (and rather incorrect) fix is to merely push the input fader down for that source – thus limiting the incoming flow.

Adjusting a low flowing source, however, is a bit more difficult – one can only "open the dam" so far by pushing the associated input fader up as far as it will go. And again, the technique is flawed.

Understand that audio sources differ in terms of their relative origin signal strength. **Line sources**, like audio servers, have relatively strong signals from the get-go. The signal from a microphone (**Mic sources**

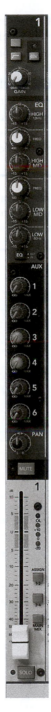

Figure 2.3 Audio Board Input Fader

(Courtesy Mackie)

monitors would be in the), on the other hand, can be as much as 50dBu weaker than a Line source at the point of origin.

In order to balance all of this out, consoles will have a knob near the top of the fader strip labeled "**Line/Mic**" or "**Trim**" or "**Gain**." By adjusting the Gain knob, the incoming signal or flow of an audio source can be increased or reduced as needed. In pre-production, the audio operator will balance out the incoming signals to an equivalent measure (ideally an average peak of –20dBu). Thus, input meters that measure incoming flow are a vital part of pre-production audio checks.

WARNING: a risk of using too much Gain to amplify low audio levels is that any noise or artifacts in the audio signal will be amplified as well. Gain cannot really "fix" audio that was acquired at a relatively low level.

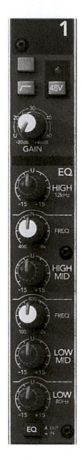

Figure 2.4 Top of Input Fader Showing Phantom Power, Gain control, and Equalizer (Courtesy Mackie)

SIGNAL PROCESSING ON THE FADER STRIP

Audio consoles will usually permit some signal processing of the audio sources beyond the raw manipulation of signal strength. Simple **equalization (EQ)** tasks are usually handled either on the fader strip itself (with knobs dedicated to groups of frequency ranges – such as low, middle, and high) or by using an equalizer that can be accessed in another manner. One very common variation uses a **select** button (located on each fader) that permits the utilization of one EQ control interface for the entire console (a **common control interface**). An equalizer merely boosts or reduces signal strength within a given set (or group) of frequencies.

Filtering, if available on your console, will either be located on the fader strip itself or by using the select switch variation coupled with the common control interface. A filter marks a specific frequency and then reduces all signals below or above the mark. Filters are sometimes referred to as cutoffs (low pass cutoff, high pass cutoff).

Depending on the manufacturer of your console, other controls may be located on the fader strip. **Solo** allows you to isolate and listen to a given source for monitoring purposes without affecting the overall mix of Audio Program. Solo is useful, for example, in adjusting a troublesome source while in the middle of a live program. **Pan** is another common control. Pan allows you to "send" a given source Left or Right in the overall output mix. Using Pan, one could "send," if you will, a mic source only to the right channel of Audio Program. The **Mute** control allows you to instantly turn source flow on or off without manipulating the fader knob. Mute is sometimes referred to as a "cut" switch.

Phantom Power is a feature built into many audio consoles. Phantom Power (48 volts of Direct Current (DC) sends power back down the input line (on the grounding wire) and is used to power capacitor microphones without the need for a battery.

In addition to the input fader strips and the Master Fader, the audio console will likely contain controls that adjust monitor volume in the Control Room and (if so equipped) in the Studio. Monitor volume will need to be adjusted in the Control Room largely to the level preferred by the Director. In the typical newscast, studio monitors would be in the "off" position as they are not needed and would create a feedback loop through the open anchor microphones (unless a clever engineer used a **mix-minus** set-up to feed the studio). The mix-minus technique can also be used to feed program audio to a person reporting from a **remote** site (the program mix minus the remote mic).

Another audio feed that is required to be patched back into the studio is known as **IFB (interruptible foldback or interruptible feedback)**. The plastic "bug" that you can see hooked into the ear of the anchor allows the anchor to monitor Audio Program during the show. The anchors can hear the entire program mix (sometimes including their own microphone and

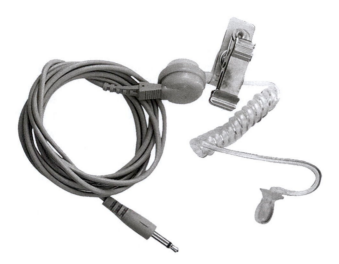

Figure 2.5 IFB Earset

(Courtesy Videndum Production Solutions, Inc.)

sometimes excluding their own microphone – see mix minus) and can, therefore, monitor remote feeds and any pre-recorded material as it is played back
in the show. The important part of IFB is the "interruptible" feature. The IFB
allows anyone in the control room (usually a producer or director) to speak
directly to the anchor through the system. In doing so, a producer or director
could alert the anchor to a breaking news item or to some other change in the
program. IFB is also called "switched" talkback.

Studio Audio

The task of hooking up and connecting microphones in the studio is often
shared with the Floor Director or an Audio Assistant (A2).

MICROPHONES AND SOUND CHECK

Microphone Placement

The procedure for proper microphone placement is determined, to some
extent, by what the anchor happens to be wearing on any given day. The
primary objective is to mount the microphone unobtrusively, yet close
enough to the mouth of the talent to get a strong audio signal. An easy rule
to follow uses the distance between the thumb and pinky (outstretched
like a heavy metal rocker), where the thumb is placed on the anchor's chin
(anchor head is level) and the hand rotated so that the pinky points to a
spot on the chest of the talent. A mic placement in this general area (horizontally) should be adequate to acquire a good signal.

The second objective is to "dress" the cable that connects the micro-phone head to the microphone power pack. Often, this will require the talent to "drop" the power pack down the back (or front) of the shirt – the microphone head can then **"sneak"** between shirt-front buttons to ride on a lapel or tie – or to mount on the collar. In any case, the cable between the microphone head and microphone power pack should be hardly seen. The power pack should be mounted on a belt, pocket, or on the belt line of the pants (to the rear is best).

At this point, the Floor Director should be sure to turn the microphone power pack "on." If the mics are wireless, the signal should now be trans-mitting to the audio area in the control room. If the mics are not wireless, they will need to be connected to the appropriate patch panel via an XLR cable or hooked into an **audio snake** at the designated terminal.

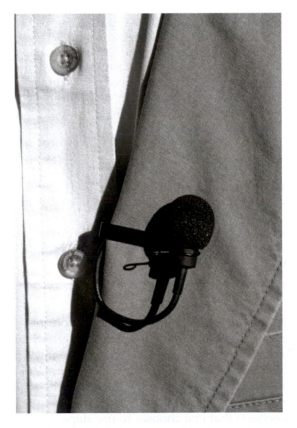

Figure 2.6 Properly Mounted Lavaliere Microphone

Microphone Types and Pick-up (Polar) Patterns

An easy way to understand the world of microphones is to remember that microphones can be categorized by type (what they look like – the body style – *like the difference between a pick-up truck and a car*) and by pickup patterns (acquisition characteristics, also called the polar pattern).

The five basic **types of microphones** are:

1. **Lavalier** (most common studio microphone)
2. **Handheld** (most common field microphone)
3. **Shotgun** (long cylinder shape)
4. **Stand** or Desktop (very similar to handheld – yet not really designed to be held "in the hand")
5. **Boundary** or **Pressure Zone Microphones** (the PZM).

The five basic **pickup/polar patterns** are:

1. **Omnidirectional** – the microphone "picks-up" sound from all directions.
2. **Unidirectional or Cardioid** – the microphone "picks-up" sound in one direction (cardioid means heart-shaped).
3. **SuperCardioid** – the microphone "picks-up" sound in a unidirectional fashion that is both narrower and extended in sensitivity. An increased, amplified, or strengthened version of the Cardioid.
4. **HyperCardioid** – a "enhanced" version of the SuperCardioid with added dimension to rear sensitivity.

Note to reader regarding cardioid patterns: enhanced sensitivity to the front of the microphone; limited sensitivity to the rear of the microphone.

5. **UltraCardioid** – the microphone "picks-up" sound in a very very narrow, unidirectional fashion with extended sensitivity.

Note: microphones are manufactured in bidirectional polar patterns but these are not commonly used in typical studio, field, ENG, or EFP applications.

The primary idea to remember is that many types of microphones are manufactured and sold with different pickup patterns. Simply by looking at a microphone, one can really only identify the microphone *type*. For example, a given lavalier may be an omni ... or a uni ... or a cardioid. The technician will need to closely examine the microphone (and sometimes the owner's manual) to determine the pickup pattern.

The microphone(s) that one chooses to use depends on the production environment (studio vs. field), the type of show (genre), the number of talent positions, the design of the set, whether the talent needs to move, the type of mics available, etc. Typically, in a controlled environment like a studio, an omnidirectional lavalier would be a good choice.

Sound Check

Once the microphones are hooked-up, the Floor Director will often assist the Audio technician with microphone checks for each microphone to be used in the show. Since it is not all that common to have an audio technician in the studio during the program, the Floor Director should be prepared to solve any audio difficulties that might arise during a show. The Floor Director should have ready access to replacement microphones, batteries, and XLR cables in case instant troubleshooting is required.

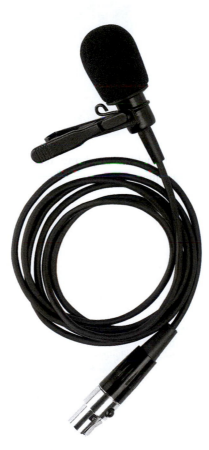

Figure 2.7 Cardioid Lavalier Microphone; Electro-Voice RE92Tx
(Courtesy Electro-Voice)

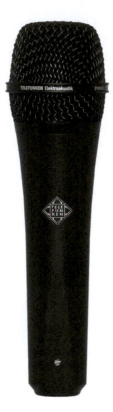

Figure 2.8 Supercardioid Handheld Microphone; Telefunken M80
(Courtesy Telefunken Elektroakustik)

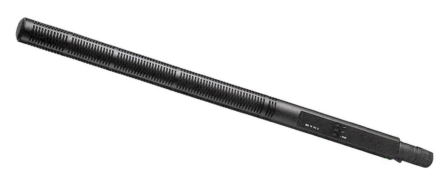

Figure 2.9 Supercardioid Shotgun Microphone; Sennheiser MKH-70
(Courtesy Sennheiser)

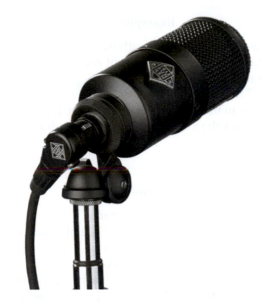

Figure 2.10 Cardioid Stand Microphone; Telefunken M82
(Courtesy Telefunken Elektroakustik)

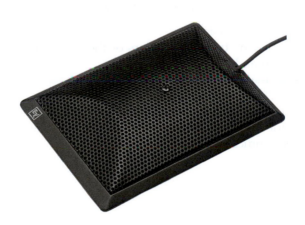

Figure 2.11 Cardioid Boundary Microphone; Electro-Voice RE90B
(Courtesy Electro-Voice)

AUDIO AND THE DIRECTOR

The directing commands that Audio must respond to are numerous. However, a good Director will always give Audio a "ready" cue of some kind and a "do it" cue of some kind. The left hand of Audio covers the Input Faders and the right hand covers the Master Fader area. Consider the following examples:

Example One

Director Says, Ready Camera One with the Mic and a Cue.

Audio identifies input fader of relevant microphone.

Audio checks that Master Fader is open.

Director Says, Take Camera One, Mic and Cue.

On the Mic command, Audio pushes input fader up (or cuts fader on) to zero mark and then adjusts fader position based on output meter indication.

Example Two

Director Says, Stand-by video clip, full-track.

Audio identifies the two input faders of the playback device.

Audio checks that Master Fader is open.

Director Says, Roll Clip, **Track**, and **Take**.

On the Track command, Audio pushes both faders up to zero mark (or cuts both faders on) and then adjusts fader position based on output meter indication.

Example Three

Director Says, Ready Music.

Audio identifies the two input faders of the music source (probably a digicart or similar audio player/server).

Audio checks that Master Fader is open.

Director Says, Go Music (or Go Sound) or Hit Music.

On the Director's command, Audio pushes "play" on the music source, pushes both faders up to zero mark, and then adjusts fader position based on output meter indication.

3

TECHNICAL
DIRECTING

INTRODUCTION

The production tasks associated with video control in the production environment is the primary responsibility of the **Technical Director (TD)**.

The primary job of the Technical Director is to operate the video switcher – thus controlling the program video that viewers see at home. The TD is located in the Control Room, usually near to the Director, and located at the video switcher. **Video program**, much like audio program, is the final compilation of video sources that is sent out for transmission or recorded.

TECHNICAL DIRECTOR/VIDEO SWITCHER

The primary responsibility of the Technical Director in a studio production environment is to operate the **video switcher**. The TD anticipates and responds to commands from the Director, activating video sources to video program as needed and on-demand. To understand the job of the TD, one must understand the basics of switcher operation.

The Video Switcher

A video switcher is a video selection device. Common video sources that the TD can select from include the studio cameras: Camera 1,

DOI: 10.4324/9780429244100-3

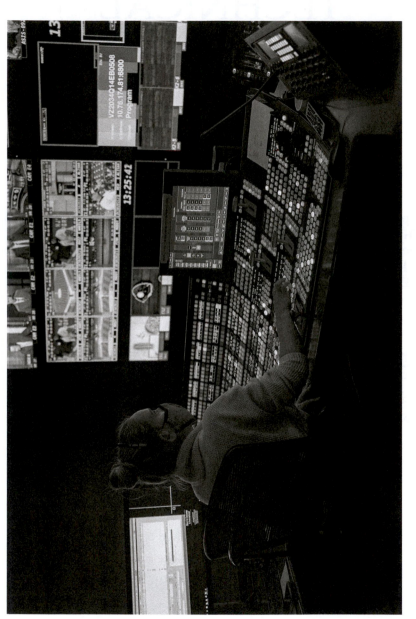

Figure 3.1 The Technical Director and the Video Switcher – ESPN Digital Center 2, Bristol, CT – April 1, 2021, MLB Opening Day

(Photo by Kelly Backus/Courtesy ESPN Images)

Camera 2, Camera 3, and so forth; the "external" playback machines for pre-recorded video clips: DDRs, video-clip and/or video file-servers; satellite feeds; microwave feeds; bonded cellular feeds; graphics computers; and, the switcher itself is a video source: **color bars**, color backgrounds, black, and depending on the model of the switcher – internal still-images, and/or pre-recorded video clips. And, it is important to remember that one could have any number of cameras, external playback machines, cellular, satellite and microwave feeds, and graphics computers, depending on the facility.

The Mix Effects Bus (M/E)

A typical video switcher will have a group of three rows of buttons located on the lower left area of the panel. Each individual row is called a Bus. A group of three busses together is called a **Mix Effects Bus (M/E).**

Many switchers will have more than one Mix Effects Bus. If your switcher has more than one M/E, they will commonly be numbered (M/E 1, M/E 2, M/E 3) and are usually color-coded.

Identifying Preview/Program/Key

For now, focus upon the M/E that is closest to the front of the console, and located nearest to the operator. The bottom row of buttons is called the **Preview Bus**. The next row up (usually the middle row) of buttons is called the **Program Bus**. The top row (if your switcher is so-equipped and most are) is called the **Key Bus**. You will note that each of the rows of buttons is identical – for example, in the bottom row, the first button might be labeled "Black." If this is the case, the first button of the second row and the first button of the third row (if your switcher is so equipped) will also be labeled "Black." Each button represents a video source that, when pressed, selects or activates that particular source in the selected bus.

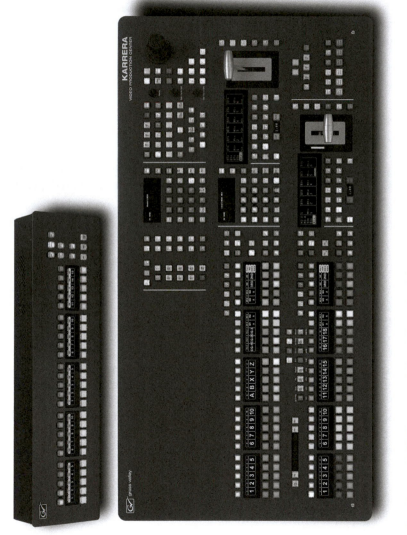

Figure 3.2 Grass Valley Karrera™ 2ME Compact Panel Video Switcher
(Courtesy Grass Valley)

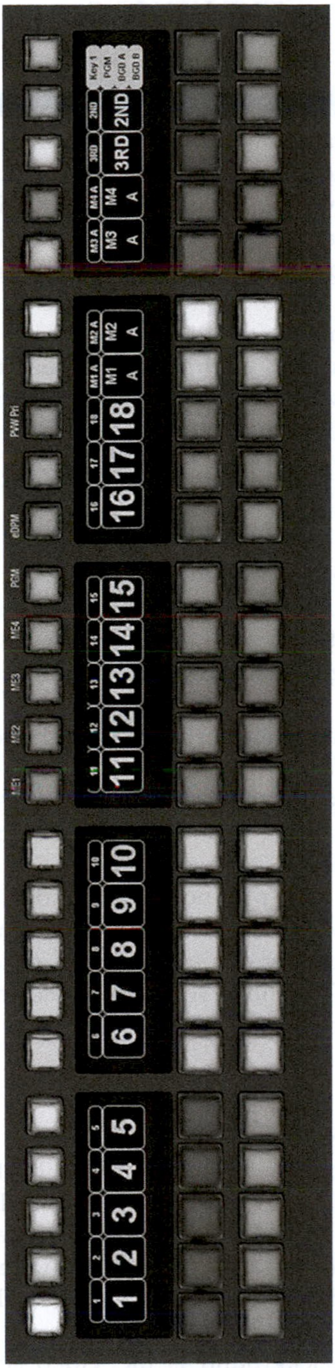

Figure 3.3 Mix Effects Bus
(Courtesy Grass Valley)

THE PREVIEW BUS, THE PROGRAM BUS, AND THE KEY BUS

The Preview Bus

When you press the button labeled "Camera 1" in the Preview Bus, then, the video signal being generated by Camera 1 appears in the Preview Monitor. If you press "Bars" in the Preview Bus, Color Bars appears in the Preview Monitor. Remember, Preview is the video signal that is "on-deck" or next.

When the Director wants to activate a signal to Preview, she will call a **Ready Cue** or a **Stand-By Cue**. For example, "ready camera one," is a command for the TD to activate Camera 1 in the Preview Bus. "Stand-by AirSpeed A," is a command for the TD to activate AirSpeed "channel" A into the Preview Bus. Savvy Directors will use the term "ready" for cameras and the term "stand-by" for pre-recorded video clips to facilitate communication with the production crew.

The Program Bus

When you press "Camera 1" in the Program Bus, the video signal being generated by Camera 1 appears in the Program Monitor. Remember that video program is the video signal that is "hot" or "live" – it is what everyone at home is watching (when the studio is live) or the video signal that is being recorded.

Therefore, it is important to be very careful with the panel buttons in the Program Bus when the facility is in live production – if you press a button in the Program Bus, the associated video source goes directly to Program. Using the Program Bus during a show is called "hot switching." The technique is not recommended.

In pre-production or post-production situations (before the show or after the show), the TD will often select directly from the Program Bus for efficiency. At these points, there is little worry of accidentally selecting the "wrong" video source. The video source selected in the Program Bus is also called the "**video background**."

The Key Bus

If your switcher is equipped with a third row of buttons in the M/E (and most switchers are), the row is called the Key Bus. The video source that is selected here will be delegated as a **Key Source**. To understand the Key Bus, one must understand what a key is. A **Key** is merely a "video layer" that is independently selected and controlled from the "video background."

The program video background is the video source selected in the Program Bus (see "The Program Bus" discussion above). The key source is the video source associated with the button selected in the Key Bus. Any video source can be a key and any video source can be the background. Therefore, any video source can be "keyed over" any other. Commonly, a graphics computer is selected as a key source.

Once selected, the material sourced from (displayed on) the graphics computer can then be keyed over the background video (perhaps the background is video sourced from a camera). For example, when an anchor's name pops up on the screen over his or her image (as acquired from the camera), the key has been activated and the key source is a graphics computer that is displaying the anchor's name "over" the camera image.

Keys get confusing. The current switcher I use can activate six independent key layers over the background at the same time (thus, the viewer at home is seeing a total of seven video sources). Yet, the total combined capability of the switcher exceeds this. And, all seven video sources are independently controlled. Also, depending on the make/model of the switcher, one can activate multiple keys in multiple M/E busses at the same time. It is possible, then, to be viewing multiple video sources at the same time in the Program Monitor. (A good example of this is "typical" CNN Headline News programming; an amazing example of this is the America's Cup coverage from early 2021).

Routing a keyed video source through a **Digital Picture Manipulator (DPM)** allows the TD to position and/or resize that image. For example, if the graphics computer is displaying a still image (a still picture) of a fire and the graphics computer is assigned to the keyer, and the keyer is sized/positioned through the DPM, it creates a quarter screen "box" effect. For now, remember that a key is a separate video source that is a video layer independently controlled from the Preview and Program busses.

Note: A **bus** is a row of buttons. Any bus can be assigned, or **delegated** to be used for different functionality. For example, the Key Bus on the switcher I currently use is located as the third row of buttons (as is typical for a Key Bus). However, the Key Bus can be delegated to control key source selection (for all six keys), record and play macros (short programs of button push sequences), and to recall panel eMems.

DVE/DPM (DIGITAL PICTURE MANIPULATOR, GRASS VALLEY)/DME (DIGITAL MULTI-EFFECTS, SONY)

No matter what you name it, the ability of the switcher to manipulate 2D images and 3D objects is one of the switcher's more notable features. **Digital Video Effects (DVE)** really began, historically, as an after-market "magic box" external to the switcher. Video signals could be routed to the DVE (often through an aux bus), manipulated (re-sized, repositioned, moved, flown about the screen, etc.), and brought back into the switcher as a new and independent video source (which could be used "straight" or as the source for a key layer (as seen in the typical over-the-shoulder "box shot").

Today, the DVE/DPM/**DME** function is internal to the switcher, and is part of the keyer. 2D effects are simple. A source is routed to or selected as the source for one of the keyers. The source is manipulated and used directly or manipulated through a sequence of recorded moves (as key-frames) and "recorded" to an eMem/effect. While 3D effects can be created in a number of different ways, a basic example would require the assignment of two video sources into two keyers, each keyer could be resized/repositioned to create a "two-box" effect.

Macros and eMems

As you might imagine, the time and effort to set up a switcher can be significant. The ability for the switcher to "remember" set-ups is the function of the **eMem** (effects memory) area. Typically located on the far right of the panel, the eMem area is essentially *a flash memory computer* controlled by a numeric keypad. While the file naming protocols will differ somewhat from manufacturer to manufacturer, essentially the operator will "learn" a panel set-up using a numeric sequence. To recall a panel set-up, the operator will recall the desired file using the same numeric sequence. On a Grass Valley switcher, the three number sequence for eMems is set up in an organizational logic known as P-B-R (page=hundreds, bank=tens, register=last digit).

eMems save and recall the state of various parts of the switcher. **Macros** remember commands (button pushes, or menu-driven commands) given to the switcher. They have separate functionality and work together; a macro can recall an eMem (button-push), and an eMem can trigger a macro.

The ability for the TD to operate the switcher efficiently is the role of a macro. As mentioned before, a macro is a short program of button push sequences. Similar to eMems, a macro *uses flash memory* to record a sequence. However, a specific macro is typically recorded to a button on one of the "available" busses. As mentioned before, the buttons in the Key Bus can be "delegated" as macro record/play buttons. Macro record/play buttons might be located in other places as well – like one of the aux busses (thus the TD can record and/or play macros from other "available" buttons on the panel).

Aux Bus

An **aux bus** is comprised of rows of buttons that are either of fixed functionality or programmable functionality. As such, an aux bus might be used to select and send a video source to any number of locations. For example, the aux bus might be set up in such a manner as to select and send a video source to one (or all) of the monitors in the studio (thus functioning as a **routing switcher**). As mentioned before, an aux bus might be used as a place to record and play macros. An aux bus might be used to send program video to a back-feed in a remote set-up. The value of the aux function, then, is the flexible (programmable) nature of these additional rows of buttons.

Signal flow: Destination/Source – All switchers perform the same functionality: if a bus has multiple functions, you must select/delegate that function/destination first, before you select the source. For example, if a Key Bus has "Key 3" selected as it's function/destination, and you want to change the source feeding Key 2, you must change the bus delegation to Key 2 first, or you will change the wrong key source.

Aux busses perform the same way. Aux busses are simply "more" switchable or programmable outputs of the switcher. For example, if you want to change the source feeding a set monitor, you must select the proper destination in the aux bus first, then the source. The destination or delegation bus is usually the row of buttons above the source bus.

FLIP-FLOP SWITCHING

In order to select a video source to Preview or to select a video source to Program, the TD merely presses the button that corresponds to the video source desired. To actually switch a live show, however, the TD will "flip-flop" switch – in other words, the TD will activate a source to Preview and then transition that source (or move that source) to Program in one of three ways: **cut**, **wipe**, or **dissolve**. The source that was in Preview goes to Program, and the source that was on Program goes to Preview – they *flip-flop*.

On most switchers the transition control area is immediately to the right of the M/E bus or Preview/Program bank that is closest to the operator. The usual set-up includes a button that is labeled "cut" next to a button labeled "auto" or "auto trans." Immediately adjacent to or (more typically) immediately above the "cut" and "auto" buttons are two more buttons: "wipe" and "mix." Commonly, a switcher will also have a "manual" **Fader Bar** located in the transition area as well.

The BKGD and Key1–6 buttons are *what* will be changed. The Cut, Auto, Mix, Wipe buttons and Lever Arm are used to determine *how* they will change.

Above the "wipe" and "mix" buttons will be a button labeled BKGD for "background" and at least one KEY button (again, the switcher I currently use has six KEY buttons). The BKGD button is normally active all the time in a basic switching exercise. The KEY button is normally not active during a basic switching exercise.

Essentially, by depressing one or the other or both, one is telling the switcher what video (the background, the key, or both) is part of the next transition. You can hold down one button, then select each additional button to **latch** them together (or punch all of the desired buttons at the same time). Thus, each button's on/off "state" will flip-flop when the next transition is activated.

Examples

If the BKGD button is selected ("on") and a transition is activated, then the background will change.

If the KEY 1 button is selected ("on") and a transition is activated, then Key 1 will activate if KEY 1 was "in preview."

If the KEY 1 button is selected ("on") and a transition is activated, then Key 1 will deactivate if KEY 1 was "in program."

> Not to confuse the reader, but consider the following idea: If all seven buttons are active (the one BKGD button, and all six KEY buttons), and the TD activates a basic cut transition, all seven video sources will change position from Preview to Program OR from Program back to Preview at the same time.

The Cut

The process to "cut" a source from Preview to Program is simple. The TD will make sure the BKGD button is active and the KEY button is not. The TD will select the source desired in the Preview Bus and press the "cut" button in the transition area. The selected source will transition (instantly) from Preview to Program.

For example, consider the following commands from a Director: "Ready Camera One," and "Take Camera One." At the "ready" cue the TD will press the Camera One button in the Preview Bus. At the "take" command, the TD will press the Cut button in the transition area. (Take is the Directing command for the TD to activate a Cut transition).

The Dissolve

The process to dissolve to a source selected in the Preview Bus is similar. The TD will make sure the BKGD button is active and none of the KEY buttons are. The TD will activate the "mix" button (this will deactivate the "wipe" button and set-up the switcher so that the next transition effect will be a dissolve). The TD will select the source desired in the Preview

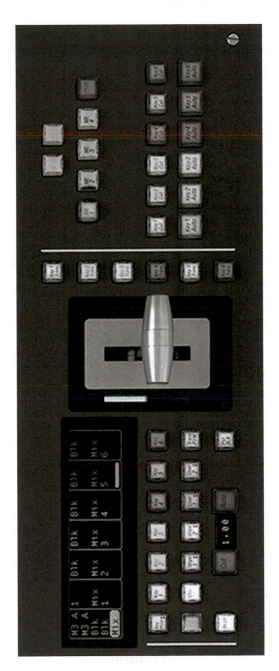

Figure 3.4 Transition area
(Courtesy Grass Valley)

Bus. At this point, the TD will either punch the "auto" button (engaging an automatic dissolve) or manually grasp the Fader Bar to pull (or push) the dissolve.

For example, consider the following commands from a Director: "Ready Camera One, we will dissolve," and "Dissolve". At the "ready" cue the TD will press the Camera One button in the Preview Bus and prepare for a dissolve. At the "dissolve" command, the TD (in this case) will punch the "auto" button.

ADDITIONAL TRANSITIONS

The Fader Bar

If the Director says, "Ready Camera One, we will dissolve, and I want you to pull (or push) it," the TD merely uses the Fader Bar instead of the "auto" button to engage the dissolve effect.

A fun note: A Grass Valley switcher Fader Bar is used to "activate" the Death Star in the very first Star Wars movie released in 1977.

A note is warranted about production terminology at this point. The command to "**fade**" is often used interchangeably with the command "dissolve." A fade indicates that the transition is to utilize the "Black" video source in a dissolve effect. A TD, then, can "fade" to Black or "fade" up from Black but cannot "fade" from Camera One to Camera Two. However, usage is particular to the Director at hand and, ultimately, will vary.

The Wipe

The final transition is the wipe. Wipes are engaged in almost the exact same manner as dissolves but carry an important extra step in the process. To engage a wipe effect to the video source selected in Preview the TD will make sure the BKGD button is active and the KEY buttons are not. The TD will activate the "wipe" button (this will deactivate the "mix" button and set up the switcher so that the next transition effect will be a wipe). The TD will now select a wipe pattern – the extra step.

Wipe Patterns

Wipe patterns determine the geometric shape of the wipe. Depending on the video switcher, numerous wipe patterns are available to select from

– circles, squares, triangles, rectangles, stars, clock arms (the Batman effect), straight line (top, bottom, left, and right), and other machine digital patterns are a few of the common ones.

Once a pattern is selected, multiple characteristics of the wipe pattern can be manipulated depending on the switcher capability (border, edge softness or hardness (blur), border thickness, border color, pattern position, rotation, rotation speed, pattern duplicates (i.e. two or more stars), aspect ratios, etc.

Once the wipe pattern and its characteristics are set, the TD will either punch the "auto" button (engaging an automatic wipe) or manually grasp the Fader Bar to pull (or push) the wipe.

For example, consider the following commands from a Director: "Ready Camera One, we will wipe," and "Wipe." At the "ready" cue the TD will press the Camera One button in the Preview Bus and prepare for the wipe. At the "wipe" command, the TD (in this case) will punch the "auto trans" button. If the Director says, "Ready Camera One, we will wipe, and I want you to pull (or push) it," the TD merely uses the Fader Bar instead of the "auto" button to engage the wipe effect.

A KEY IS A VIDEO LAYER

Keying

In order to select a key source the TD will depress the appropriate button of the desired video source in the properly delegated Key Bus. For this discussion, imagine that Camera One is in Program, Camera Two is in Preview, and the TD has selected the Graphics Computer as the Key Source.

Furthermore, assume that the name "Roger Hicks" has been typed into the Graphics Computer and that the name is centered on the computer screen on the bottom line (a "lower third"). At this point, the TD has to decide how to activate the key – how to "bring the key on" over the active program source. Even using a basic switcher, the TD may have more than one choice.

Activating a Key in the Transition Area

The key button (KEY) is located in the transition area next to the background (BKGD) button. To activate the key, the TD will need to activate the KEY button and (in this case) deactivate the BKGD button. The switcher is now set up, then, to bring on a key layer (Graphics Computer) without effecting the existing BKGD (Camera One) in Program.

At this point, the TD can "cut" the key on using the "cut" button, "dissolve" the key on, or "wipe" the key on. If the key is to be dissolved on or wiped on, the TD will need to select the effect desired (Mix or Wipe) in the transition area and either punch the "auto" button or engage the Fader Bar. To remove the key layer, the TD merely cuts, wipes, or dissolves the key source "off."

If the TD desires to transition the background video source BKGD and the key video source KEY at the same time, the TD merely activates both buttons (a double punch) at the top of the transition area. When the transition is activated (cut, wipe, or dissolve), both video sources will change at the same time. The background will change to the video source in Preview, the key will merely activate (or deactivate) as the case may be.

A Direct Access Key

Another way to activate a key is to bring the key on independent from a traditional BKGD/KEY transition. If the switcher has a small bus of dedicated key buttons near the transition area (usually just above or to the right) the TD can activate (and deactivate) key layers by pressing the desired button (probably a cut bus but sometimes a dissolve or "mix" bus AND sometimes both effects are available in separate busses). A direct access keyer will be labeled "KEY1 Cut" and/or "KEY1 Mix" (the layer will either "cut" or "dissolve" on). When activated, the key will appear, layered over the program video source. A direct key source is selected from or "assigned" from the Key Bus. **Direct access key** buttons are faster to use, because they involve fewer button presses, but they are instant, and thus, will not appear in Preview first.

DIRECTING A KEY

What Video Source Is Where?

Many switchers have more than one key available (KEY1 and KEY2 and KEY3 and so on). Remember, each is independent of the other and each is controlled in precisely the same manner. The difficult part of the process is keeping track of what video source is assigned to each keyer and which keyer is active – one or all can be "on" at the same time in any combination.

Directing a Key

When a Director wants to activate a key, the Director will convey the command to the TD in one of the following ways:

"Stand-by Downstream," and "Downstream."
Ready to Font, and "Font."
Ready to Key, and "Key."

As you can see, there is a great deal of variance on this particular directing command.

Keys can be manipulated in almost as many ways as wipe patterns. For the most part, keys will be **Fixed Linear** keys, the Key will look as the artist intended it to look, the only adjustment being *opacity* (vs. transparency), which should be set at 100 percent. Other "types" of keys include **luminance** keys and chroma keys.

Note: See Chapter 6 for more on the different types of keys.

DIRECTING THE TD

A Director should always give ready or stand-by cues prior to command cues; and, the Director must be consistent with any command language she chooses to use. With practice, then, the technicians will be able to anticipate the Director's needs.

In many news environments, the separation line between the production folks and the producing staff is not as well defined as it may need to be. Once the show begins, the technicians need to be clear of the fact that the boss is the Director, not the Producer or any other member of the producing staff. Producers need to be clear on this protocol as well and must refrain from communicating directly to any technician during an actual production.

The audio-visual requirements of every newscast will vary. Technical Directors will need to be flexible, and to some extent accommodating, in order for the production to be a success. The manner in which live feeds are handled, the procedures for breaking news, and the nuances of the facility will differ from station to station. The most important idea to keep in mind is that success is really defined by the production procedures in place – the more practiced and consistent the production protocols are, the more technically complicated a show can be. Ideally, then, any deviance from regular protocols should be well-rehearsed prior to transmission. A good TD is *pro*active, not *re*active.

4

LIGHTING AND SETS

INTRODUCTION

Set design and lighting design are two sides of the same coin. While the traditional mode of set design begins with an assessment of program needs (the type of show, the number of talent), lighting design is a somewhat constricted art due to the specific technical requirements needed to create the video image. Both topics are extensive in their own right and entire courses are based on each. The goal of this chapter is to introduce each in a most basic sense and is limited. It is important to note that lighting and set design are tightly constrained by the station and/or program budget, the physical limitations of the studio, and the lighting package available for use in any given set-up.

SET PLACEMENT

One of the first considerations when undertaking the design process for a studio installed news set is the physical space of the studio itself. If the studio is to be dedicated to the news program, and no other programs are to utilize the space, the set can pretty much encompass the entire space. If this is the case, the best possible positioning for the news set may be the middle of the studio. The reasoning behind this "centered" placement might not be completely obvious. A centered set increases the number of possible camera angles (360 degree coverage) and greatly increases the possibilities for lighting placement and coverage. Additionally, a centered set creates a great deal of visual depth to nearly every camera composition – an added bonus.

However, most studios will need to accommodate at least one other program and so the news set will need to "share" the space. The choice will need to be made, then, between parking the set along a wall or into one

DOI: 10.4324/9780429244100-4

of the corners. The advantage to using a flat wall stems from maximizing studio space for other program set-ups. At least three walls in most studios will be usable; therefore, one could "set" three separate shows along them. In this set-up, cameras can "cover" 180 degrees of each set; and, the lighting design is still fairly flexible. However, a *major disadvantage* exists within this construction – visual depth is compromised (and therefore a key ingredient **(Z-Axis)** to visual interest is lost). In other words, the set appears flat.

A nice compromise between a centered set and a set placed along the wall of the studio is corner placement. When a set is parked into a corner, visual depth is somewhat recreated naturally. Furthermore, at least two other corners of the studio are left for other set-ups; and, in a typical news set-up, the chroma key area can be naturally joined to the set along an adjacent flat wall space. The disadvantages of corner placement really stem from camera angle flexibility and the generation of some limitation on back lighting placements. If the set is placed in a studio corner, yet well distanced from the cyc, some of these limitations can be minimized.

RISERS, FLATS, DESK

The traditional news set is constructed on an 8 to 10 inch platform made up of **risers**. Risers are merely used to boost the set into the air so that a typical camera angle will remain lens-to-eye-level to the anchors. Risers permit the camera operators to stand normally behind the cameras for the duration of the program. Risers will typically be carpeted in order to deaden sound and to enhance appearance. In design terms, risers can also add an element of visual focus to the set.

Placed on top of the risers will be the ubiquitous **news desk**. No part of the set says "news" more clearly than the desk. Perhaps no other set element has been fussed with as much and as frequently as the desk. No matter. Whatever the shape, color, size, or material, the news desk will ideally accommodate up to four anchors at a time (news, news, sports, weather) and must provide a comfortable spot for at least two (the news anchors – as the weather anchor can merely "lean in" on the desk.

The sports anchor will sometimes sit along the edge of the desk or may deliver the sports segment from some other dedicated spot in the studio or the sports area of the newsroom. In some colleges and universities, the news desk is not used in order to prevent new reporters from leaning and to encourage good posture. On a few of the national network newscasts, the desk is abandoned for a standing delivery (and perhaps to encourage good posture).

The background of a news set is often made up of a wall of panels called **flats**. While it is uncommon to find a newscast that does not use a flat wall, some sets permit the viewer to "see through" to the newsroom, or merely permit the background to be a clean view of the studio curtain or cyc. For those news programs that do use a flat wall, the sky is the limit.

The **duratran**, a back-lit translucent photograph of a cityscape, landmark, or other bit of the local geography, is sometimes embedded in the wall of flats. Video monitors in any number, shape, and combination, columns of light encased in plastic, logos (painted, projected, or video), book cases, woodwork, maps, glass, chrome, steel, and just about anything else you can think of become news set backgrounds. The cost of a new news set ranges from very little into the millions.

VIRTUAL SETS AND VISUALIZATION WALLS

Virtual sets are also commonly in use (primarily in Asia). A virtual set is a computer-generated background (the chroma key effect is used to "layer" the camera images over the background graphic(s)). Some virtual sets are "active" backgrounds – perspectives and angles can be manipulated based on data provided by pan/tilt/zoom computers on the cameras.

In order to deploy a virtual set, a significant area of the studio will need to be dedicated to a larger vertical surface where the chroma key effect can be deployed. A large chroma key colored curtain or fabric wall might be used. Another option is to purchase and install a large chroma key colored hard cyc. Even today, unfortunately, the use of virtual sets still appears rather fake – similar to poor CGI (computer generated imagery) in film. Unless the keying is nearly perfect, the viewer can "tell" the set is an effect.

One very new (and still very expensive) method to get around the limitations of virtual sets is the use of "tiled" LED monitors, called a visualization wall.

A visualization wall is a huge LED monitor that is made from stacking (vertically and horizontally) smaller LED units (called "tiles") together. The Sony system uses crystal micro-led (CLED) "tiles" that are about 16 inches wide, 18 inches tall, and 4 inches deep.

The tiles can be combined (stacked) in just about any shape one can dream up (traditional monitor shapes like rectangles, squares, staircase shapes, lines, crosses, x shapes, or even off-set (like pixel grids). The technology can be scaled to enormous sizes – a wall in Singapore built by LG is 194 feet wide and 50 feet tall.

So ... the usefulness of a visualization wall as a virtual set is logical. What is interesting at this point is that the camera manufacturers (the Sony VENICE camera is an example) are combining the two technologies so that when a Sony camera is shooting "against" a Sony visualization wall, additional effects may be added.

The very newest technology for visualization walls utilizes curved tiles to create a surround effect similar to what a viewer experiences in an IMAX theatre. Visualization walls that "bend" in this manner can be

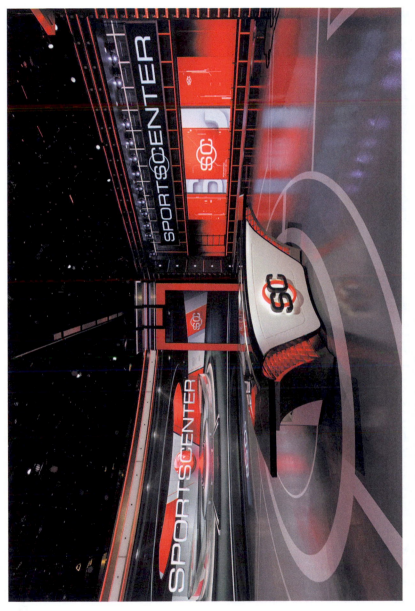

Figure 4.1 Bristol, CT – September 8, 2022 – Studio X: the SportsCenter set

(Photo by Kelly Backus/Courtesy ESPN Images)

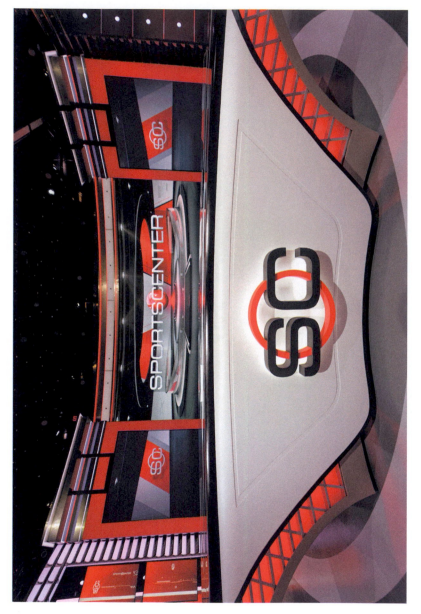

Figure 4.2 Bristol, CT – September 8, 2022 – Studio X: SportsCenter set, close-up of desk
(Photo by Kelly Backus/Courtesy ESPN Images)

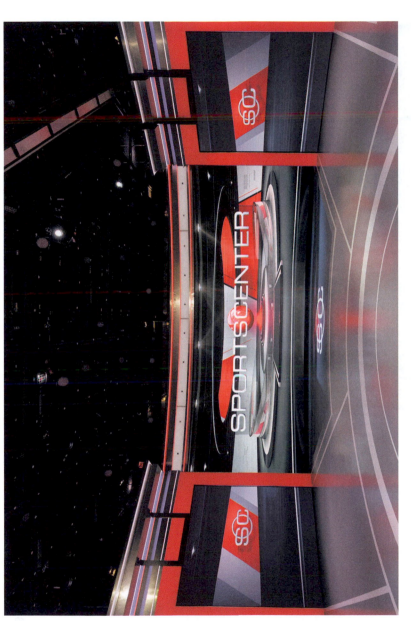

Figure 4.3 Bristol, CT – September 8, 2022 – Studio X: SportsCenter set Video Wall (48′w x 17′h) and the Video Floor (41′w x 17′d)

(Photo by Kelly Backus/Courtesy ESPN Images)

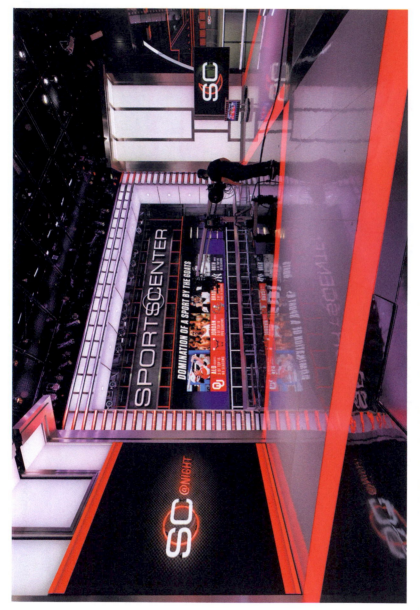

Figure 4.4 Bristol, CT – June 4, 2022 – Studio X: SportsCenter set with camera operator
(Photo by Kelly Backus/Courtesy ESPN Images)

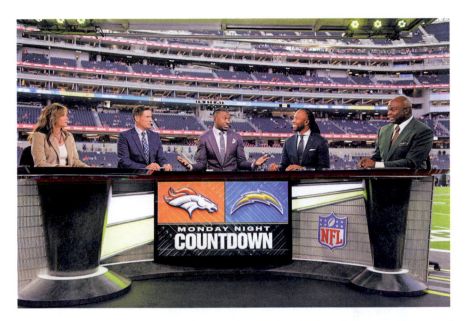

Figure 4.5 Los Angeles, CA – October 17, 2022 – SoFi Stadium, on the set of Monday Night Countdown

(Photo by Scott Clarke/Courtesy ESPN Images)

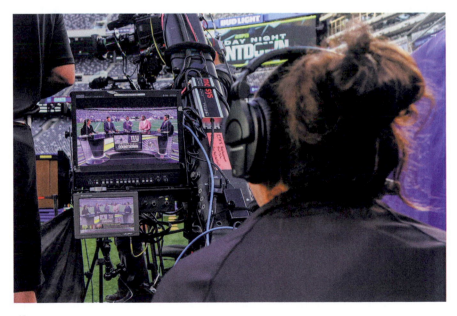

Figure 4.6 East Rutherford, NJ – September 26, 2022 – MetLife Stadium, on the set of Monday Night Countdown

(Photo by Gabriella Ricciardi/Courtesy ESPN Images)

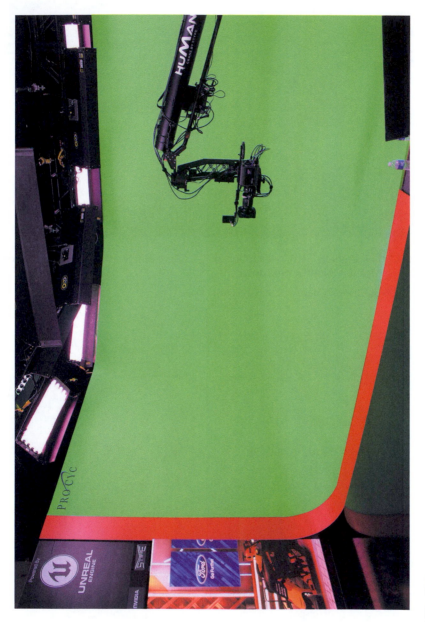

Figure 4.7 Pro Cyc

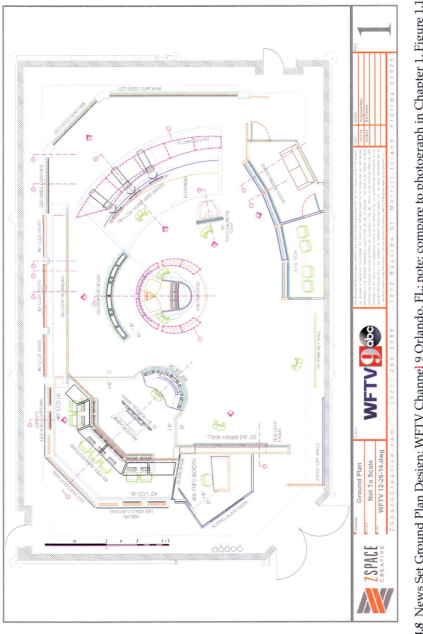

Figure 4.8 News Set Ground Plan Design; WFTV Channel 9 Orlando, FL; note: compare to photograph in Chapter 1, Figure 1.1 (Courtesy Glenn Anderson, Z Space Creative)

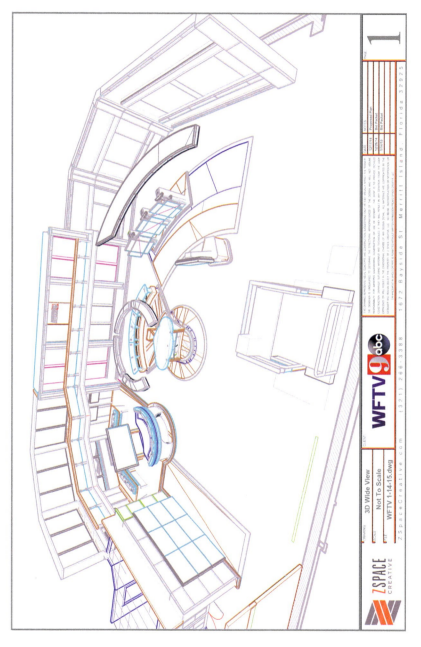

Figure 4.9 News Set 3D Wireframe; WFTV Channel 9 Orlando, FL; note: compare to photograph in Chapter 1, Figure 1.1
(Courtesy Glenn Anderson, Z Space Creative)

shaped into circles or spheres in any combination of convex or concave applications.

> *Note*: while not yet deployed, the utilization of visualization walls to replace projection in traditional movie theatre environments is a very real possibility.

THE WEATHER WALL

Adjacent to the news set will be an area dedicated to delivering the weather forecast. Either a chroma key wall or chroma key colored cyc are typically utilized in order for the weather anchor to appear to "float" in front of the weather graphics. The only real set-design consideration for the weather area concerns monitor placement and access to the computer that holds and reads the graphics sequence.

Usually, monitors will be placed around the chroma key wall in order for the weather anchor to see themselves in relation to the graphics (the combined feed). The combined feed can also be routed to the teleprompter units on the front of the cameras. In some fancier set-ups, the chroma key wall is bound or "framed" by flats or is embedded within the flat wall. Access (typically wireless) to the computer that holds the sequence of weather graphics is important in order for the weather anchor to make changes or to intervene in the sequence playback.

Yet again, the advent of the visualization wall is beginning to replace the traditional use of chroma key in this application. The weather anchor can simply stand in front of an appropriately sized visualization wall and change the graphics as needed.

Light + Set + Graphics = Look

In nearly all set design considerations for a typical affiliate newscast, a design consultant or broadcast design company will be contracted to design a "look" for the program, and to handle the construction and installation of the set and lighting package. In some cases, a graphics package (logos, colors, fonts, animations) may also be created specific to a show, station, and/or network.

Ed Luther, the Drafting and Construction Manager of Broadcast Design International, Inc. describes the Set Design process:

1. Input meeting with client: Find out the station's goals, production needs, budget, and timeline.
2. Develop floor plan to establish camera shots and traffic flow: Design floor plan to ascertain good geometry for camera placement relative to backgrounds.
3. Presentation of CAD shots and color renderings: Demonstrates how the set will look – the color scheme and materials.
4. Design approval and acceptance of the contract: Usually occurs after some design tweaks are made following client feedback.
5. Construction, installation, and lighting of set: The sets are constructed in (generally) modular pieces in one of our shops. The set is then shipped and our install team goes to the station's studio for final assembly.
6. On-Air Premiere as per client schedule: Our lighting director and project manager conduct rehearsals with the client prior to the Air Date.

LIGHTING

At the time a television studio is constructed, an important piece of the overall design and layout will concern the lighting package to be installed. In a permanent set installation, where the studio is dedicated only to the newscast (or some other program), the lighting package is often customized to (and purchased with) the news set. However, it is also common to find a studio with a general lighting package that can be used for a variety of program needs, and that can be adapted for different uses.

Electrical Service (U.S. Only)

The lighting package in any given studio begins with the electrical service to the lighting system. Studio lighting systems (halogen) used to require two to four times the amount of electricity that is required for a stand-alone, single family home. For example, it was not uncommon to service a typical studio with as much as 600 amps of conditioned power (electricity "fed" through a machine that attenuates voltage fluctuations, filters out interference, and may also condition the waveform) – with about two-thirds of the service (400 amps) ready for active use.

In the older halogen systems, a point to remember regarding the power service is that a 2000 watt lamp (a 2K) requires an individual 20 amp circuit. (So consider that 400 amps of "active" service permits the simultaneous

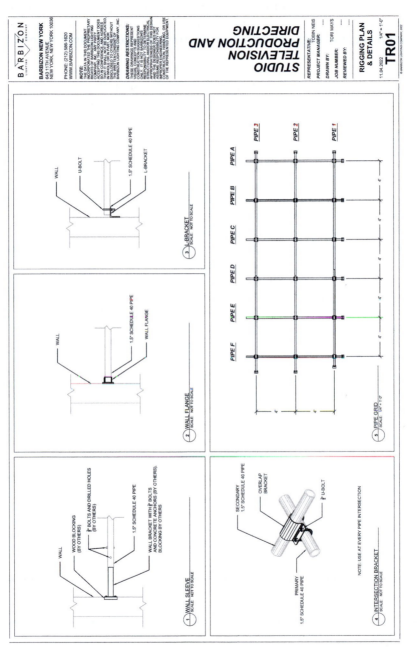

Figure 4.10 Lighting Grid Schematic
(Courtesy Barbizon Lighting Company)

illumination of twenty 20 amp circuits, each using 2000 watt lamps for a total illumination of 40,000 watts of lighting power).

However, the advent of LED lighting systems has significantly changed the equation (for the better). Unless one is working in an older halogen environment, 100 amps of standard electrical service is more than adequate to handle the lighting load in an LED environment.

Consider that a 1000 watt lamp (a 1K) in a halogen environment required an individual 10 amp circuit. In an LED environment, the equivalent fixture only uses about one-fifth the wattage (200 watts) and would only require 2 amps to operate.

THE LIGHTING GRID

The grid of pipes suspended from the ceiling of the studio is called the lighting grid. The lighting grid is made up of pipes called **battens**. In professional installations, the lighting grid is rigid and fixed.

Each individual light that hangs from the grid is called a lighting instrument. In a halogen environment, the grid will be serviced with a number of 20 amp "outlets" that hang from pigtails (short extension cables) connected to the electric system of the studio. In an LED environment, traditional electrical outlets are typically located in wiring chases (long metal boxes) that run parallel to the grid. The chases also house the network wiring and network ports for each instrument (DMX is the network – more on DMX in moment).

The lighting grid will ideally be located fairly high from the studio floor to permit as much working headroom as possible for the set installation and to allow for more flexibility with lighting placement. In order to access a fixed grid, the studio will be equipped with non-conductive ladders, a rolling ladder/platform of some fashion, or a scissor lift.

WARNING: Be aware that lighting tasks are potentially the most dangerous in the studio environment. The risk of injury or death from electrocution or from working well off of the ground is very real; and, in the case of a scissor lift system, a moment of distraction can easily result in a severed limb.

WARNING: Halogen lights become very hot very fast – wear gloves as needed. Never touch a bare halogen light bulb in a studio environment – the oil from your skin will cause the bulb to explode or otherwise fail.

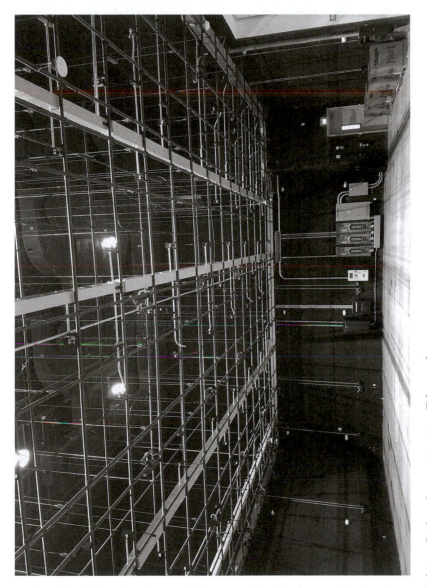

Figure 4.11 Lighting Grid under construction; Telemundo
(Courtesy Barbizon Lighting Company)

Flood Lights and Spot Lights

The lighting instruments are easily classed into two groups – **flood lights** and **spot lights**. Spot lights are a group of lighting instruments that generate a stream of light waves that are parallel and close together. The light is intense, carries a good distance, and can be harsh-looking – shadows associated with this type of light are hard-edged.

Flood lights generate light that is soft-looking, perhaps flat, in that the light waves generated by floods are not parallel or close together. Flood lights are harder to control than spot lights and do not carry as far or with as much intensity as spot lights. A wide variety of instruments from numerous manufacturers are available on the market; and the following listing of instruments is not exhaustive.

SPOT LIGHTS

Fresnels

The workhorse of the television studio is a spot light called a **fresnel**. Shaped like a large tin can, fresnels are sometimes called "cans" or "an ace," and are commonly accessorized with four black metal panels on the front called barn doors. Fresnels come in different sizes and the size of the can indicates wattage – the larger the light, the higher the wattage.

A legacy halogen studio will commonly have at least two sizes of fresnel instruments. The most common lighting set-up would include the 1000 watt fresnel (1K) as the primary type of fresnel and then include a complement of lower wattage lights (500s, 650s, or 750s). Older studios will more than likely have a few 2000 watt (2K) monsters in the grid – and these should be handled with care as they are quite heavy.

An LED studio will have the equivalent. At least two sizes of fresnels are common (1K equivalents and 500w equivalents). Note: remember the one-fifth rule: a halogen 1K is equivalent to the 200w LED; a halogen 500w is equivalent to the 100w LED).

Fresnels are primarily used for lighting people, yet are also commonly used for illuminating the set or creating special lighting effects. Fresnels have a special lens that allows for the light beam to focus. The lamp and reflector move along an internal track that "spots" or "floods" the lighting output. Therefore, fresnels are focusing beam lighting instruments.

Ellipsoidals

Another spot light that is common is called an **ellipsoidal**. Shaped like a long narrow tube, ellipsoidals are sometimes called lekos as "lekolite" was the name given to the instrument by the manufacturer. Ellipsoidals are not often used for illuminating people but are, rather, an effects light often used for sets, props, or special effects.

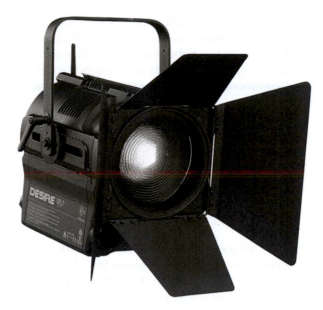

Figure 4.12 ETC Desire™ Fresnel with barndoors

(Courtesy Electronic Theatre Controls and Barbizon Lighting Company)

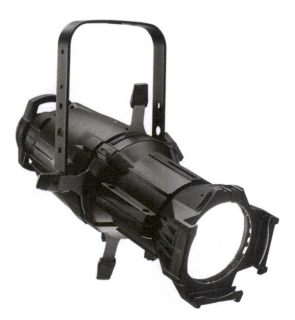

Figure 4.13 ETC Source Four™ Ellipsoidal

(Courtesy Electronic Theatre Controls and Barbizon Lighting Company)

Ellipsoidals contain internal shutters that permit the light to be shaped into patterns and other geometric shapes. Ellipsoidals can also accept pre-cut "gobos" that can project just about any two- dimensional pattern you can imagine (often a logo). Ellipsoidals are designed in multiple wattage set-ups, but are commonly 750 watt instruments (halogen) or approximately 150 watt (LED).

FLOOD LIGHTS

Flood lights are used to illuminate large areas of the studio with a soft, flat quality of light.

Scoops

An older ("legacy") halogen flood light that still may be found in older studios is the "scoop." As the name suggests, the **scoop** looks like a large metal bowl with a high output lamp in the bottom. Scoops are often used for increasing the amount of base light on a set, merely notching up the overall illumination of a given set-up.

SoftLight/Softbox/Panel

The **softlight** or **softbox** is perhaps the more common type of flood light in use in a modern studio. Softboxes, as the name suggests, are box-shaped lighting instruments that usually contain multiple lamps.

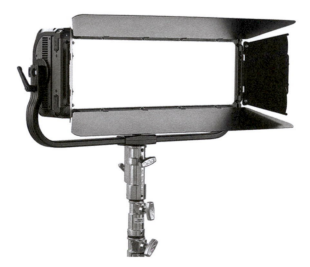

Figure 4.14 ETC fos/4 Small Panel (softbox/softlight)

(Courtesy Electronic Theatre Controls and Barbizon Lighting Company)

The LED equivalent of the softbox is called a **panel**. Panels are manufactured in numerous sizes (rectangular in shape) and provide large areas of base light or fill light.

Cyc Lights

The **cyc light** itself comes in a few variations – the **ground row** (a strip of lights), an individual cyc light (positioned on the ground washing upward), or **sky cycs** (a small softlight mounted to the grid that washes from top to bottom). Cyc lights are available in halogen or LED.

Broads

Broads (legacy) refer to flood lights that contain a two-prong halogen lamp fixed between two reflectors. While the usual spot for a **Broad** is on the grid, it is not uncommon to see a Broad light floor mounted (or on tripod-like floor mounts called C-Stands). Broads are available in halogen or LED.

Fixed Focal Length Lights

Parabolic Aluminum Reflector lights **(PARS)** are lighting instruments that are of a "fixed" throw or spread. PARs are manufactured, however, all along the continuum between spot and flood lights. PARS are available in halogen or LED.

For example, PARS can be purchased as Wide Flood lights (WFLs) and Very Narrow Spot lights (VNSP) – just remember, the beam spread is fixed. It is not uncommon to find PARS mounted in banks (groups) in order to create very powerful sources of light (usually on-location and more rarely in studio situations).

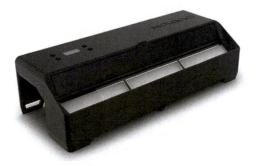

Figure 4.15 Chauvet Ovation CYC 1

(Courtesy Chauvet Professional and Barbizon Lighting Company)

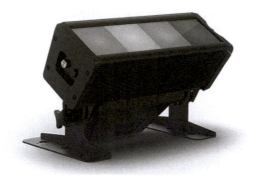

Figure 4.15a Chauvet COLORado Solo Batten 4

(Courtesy Chauvet Professional and Barbizon Lighting Company)

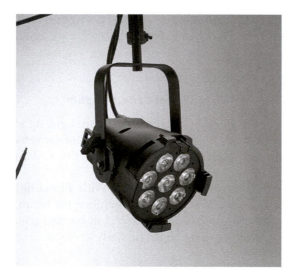

Figure 4.16 ETC ColorSource PAR

(Courtesy Electronic Theatre Controls & Barbizon Lighting Company)

Halogen – Fluorescent – LED

The type of bulb found in a lighting instrument will vary. Traditionally, halogen lamps have been used in lighting instruments for two reasons. First, halogen bulbs generate a significant amount of measurable light per input watt (a nice bang for the buck). Second, halogen bulbs are widely available. The halogen bulb, however, has a few disadvantages. A halogen bulb gets very, very hot. A large number of halogen bulbs, illuminated at the same time, will heat up a studio in minutes (thus, powerful HVAC systems are necessary to avoid cooking the talent). Halogen bulbs do not have a long life; and, halogen bulbs do not sustain "shock" very well (these bulbs are not very durable and will not tolerate rough handling). Halogen bulbs also "eat" electricity.

Lighting instruments with fluorescent bulbs became popular in the late 1990s. And, the advantages are obvious: the lamps are more durable, the quality of the light is soft, the lamps do not get very hot, and, the lamps use less electricity. However, the lamps do not generate a significant amount of measurable light.

Thus, a fluorescent lighting instrument must be located very close to the object of illumination (the lighting target). Therefore, one cannot effectively mount a fluorescent light directly on a lighting grid. Extension poles were required to move the instrument down from the grid and closer to the lighting target. Following this downward positioning, a whole host of problems ensue. The lights tend to "get in the shot." Set materials (especially flats) cannot be moved in the studio easily without the risk of collision. Rolling ladders cannot be moved in the studio easily without the risk of collision. Finally, the trend of increasing image resolution – SDTV (480) to HDTV (720 and 1080) to UHDTV (2160) – requires a commensurate increase in lighting output that fluorescent illumination cannot meet. Fluorescent lighting is no longer common.

Enter the LED.

As of this writing (late 2022) LED lamps are exploding in popularity and are quickly becoming "standard." Simply put, LED lamps give excellent light output per input watt, do not get as hot as halogen lamps (in fact LEDs burn "cold"), and are available in a variety of styles (including fresnels, ellipsoidals, and panels/softboxes). LEDs have a comparable "throw" with halogen lamps (thus one can mount them directly on the grid). LED fixtures can be more expensive. However, the cost-saving is realized over time (less electricity, less HVAC, etc.).

A Word about Color Temperature

So … legacy lighting systems (halogen) give off a warmer, yellow light. And if desired, LED lighting systems can be designed to simulate the halogen look. The color temperature of the light is about 2800 degrees kelvin. The reason this is a "big deal" is that video shot in a studio at 2800K does not match video shot in daylight.

The color temperature of daylight is about 5600 degrees kelvin (a colder and "bluer" light). So … the problem is that the color "white" on video captured in a halogen studio at 2800K is different than the color "white" on video acquired outside (5600K).

One of the huge benefits of LED is that most lighting instruments (if not all LED fixtures nowadays) are adjustable. Early LED lights could either be purchased as 2800K or 5600K (one had to choose). Again, most lights that are available today can be adjusted.

PARAMETERS AND DMX LIGHTING CONTROL

A lighting instrument that simply turns on and off and is dimmable is essentially a single parameter light. A vast majority of the lights in television studio lighting are single parameter (on/off; dimmable; perhaps a focusing beam feature like most of the Fresnels). A few lighting instruments are multi-parameter. In addition to the basics, these lights can change color; are color temperature adjustable; strobe; or move (tilt, pan, rotate, etc.). The parameter characteristics of a given lighting instrument are called its "personality."

So ... what is DMX? **DMX** stands for **digital multiplex**. DMX lighting control is best understood in that each lighting instrument is basically a location with a unique address on an inline network (just as computers on a network are assigned Internet Protocol addresses such as 111.222.333.444).

DMX allows for each lighting instrument to be programmed in terms of functionality (what it does), sequencing (when it does it), synchronizing (how it relates to other lighting instruments or other machines on the network). DMX also allows for lighting instruments to be daisy-chained on the network to form a channel. Of course, the programming may be saved in a show file (just like pretty much anything else nowadays). The logic is channel, scene, sequence. A collection of sequences is a show.

The brain of the DMX network is the lighting board. The lighting board is where the technician responsible for the lighting can program and control the network. The board may be controlled manually or to some extent automated (tied to trigger cues – sound cues, time cues, and so forth). Often, the board is programmed in such a manner that the complexity of any lighting changes is embedded as scenes in a sequence and the technician simply manually triggers the next scene (like a playlist).

LIGHTING STRATEGY

Once a set has been designed, manufactured, and constructed in the studio, a lighting strategy or design will need to be created – if it has not already been established. It is very common for a lighting strategy is to be created alongside and at the same time as the set design. Often, a lighting designer is contracted for this type of work. However, the basics of lighting design are straightforward.

Two very basic and common approaches to lighting are to either follow a **three-point** lighting strategy or to pursue a **"bank"** or flood lighting strategy within a given set-up. As the name suggests, three-point lighting utilizes three lighting instruments for each talent position on a set. The set itself and any effects lights are added only after the talent positions are taken care of. Bank lighting is altogether different. The entire set is ringed with soft flood lights in a "bank" technique. The talent positions are merely included within the ring and the entire set will appear even (and flat and boring).

The primary advantage of three-point lighting is control. Each talent position can be adjusted without influencing the overall lighting set-up. The primary advantage of bank lighting is that the talent can be blocked (or moved) anywhere on the set, and look the same. Three-point lighting generally requires more lighting instruments.

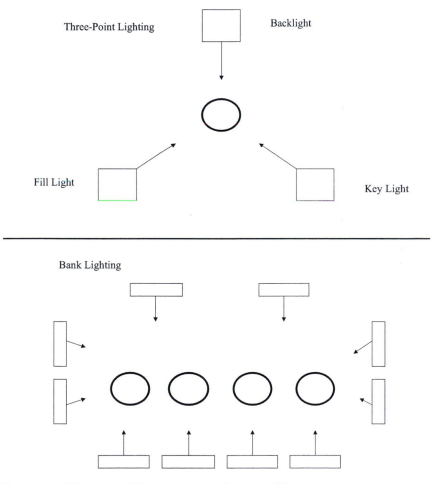

Figure 4.17 Schematics of three-point, triple key, and bank

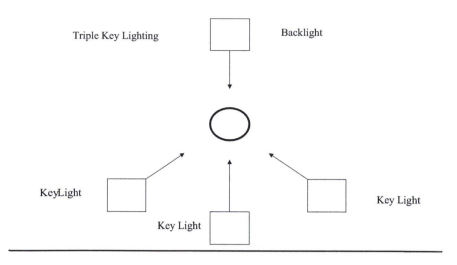

Figure 4.17a Schematics of three-point, triple key, and bank

THREE-POINT LIGHTING

Key Light

Each talent position on the set will be targeted with three (and sometimes more) lighting instruments. The first of these is the **key** light. The key light is located 45 degrees up, out, and to the left of the talent position. To find the location of the key light, merely sit at the talent position (precisely where the talent is to sit) and hold your left arm straight out from your body. Then, move the arm to the left 45 degrees and up to the grid 45 degrees – the batten position you are pointing to is the location for the key light.

A common instrument to use as a key light is a 1000 watt Fresnel or the LED equivalent. To aim the light, illuminate it and fully focus the lamp (spot it) to create a hot spot (an intense circle of light). Tilt and pan the instrument to bring the hot spot to rest on the left-center portion on the face of the talent. Lock the position.

To tune the lamp, use a **light meter** to adjust the incident light reading to a **footcandle** reading appropriate for your studio (this will depend on the type of cameras your studio is using). For example, adjust the key to 120 footcandles by defocusing (flooding) the fresnel. Once a reading of 120 footcandles is reached, adjust the **barndoors** (if equipped) on the front of the light to control **spill** (try to only light the talent). If you wind up with a shadow "climbing" the background, you will more-than-likely need to move the light forward for a steeper angle of attack.

A Quick Word about Tuning

One modern issue concerning tuning lights is the ever increasing resolution of the video image. The more scan lines one is dealing with and the number of pixels per line necessitates that more light will be required to create an acceptable image. When digital video was first released the protocol was 480p; and, 120 footcandle averages off of each light was adequate. As the protocols have increased (720p; 1080i and 1080p; 4K or 2160p; 8K or 4320p; and now 16K or 8640p), the amount of light needed from each instrument has also increased.

Fill Light

The second lighting instrument in three-point lighting is the **fill** light. Two instruments are ideal for use as fill lights in a studio set-up and each for entirely different reasons. A softbox or panel will provide an excellent fill source that will not overpower the key light. However, a softbox cannot be tuned as precisely as a fresnel without moving the lighting instrument (or the talent). A key light matched (1000 watt or equivalent) or a lesser wattage fresnel can be used to good effect as a fill light. Diffusion material (metal screening to cut down the amount of light, or **Tough Spun**, a white fabric to diffuse the light) can be used to soften the light if desired.

The fill light is placed 45 degrees up, out, and to the right of the talent position. To find the location of the fill light, merely sit at the talent position (precisely where the anchor is to sit) and hold your right arm straight out from your body. Then, move the arm to the right 45 degrees and up to the grid 45 degrees – the batten position you are pointing to is the location for the fill light.

After hanging the light in position, focus the light to a hot spot and aim the spot to the right-center of the talent's face. Tune and barndoor the light following the procedure outlined for the key light. If a softbox, panel, or other flood light is to be used, carefully aim the light to encompass the right-center portion of the talent's face. Move the instrument away from or closer to the talent while using a light meter to attempt to match (or read slightly under) the footcandle level of the key light.

Backlight

Once the key and fill lights have been hung, aimed, and tuned, the third lighting instrument in the three-point set-up needs attention – the **backlight**. The backlight is located 45 degrees up and 90 degrees straight back from the talent position. A lower wattage fresnel is a good choice for the backlight (if the key is 1K, the backlight is ideal at 500 watts).

Hang the lamp in position, aim the hot spot to the shoulder-blade level of the talent and tune the lamp to match or read slightly under the key light (tuning the backlight need not be a precise exercise as it will not effect flesh tone). The backlight creates a visual separation of the talent from the background – creating depth and interest. More lights can be added at this point (hair lights, kickers, side lights) although all are for effect rather than primary illumination. Hair lights, for example, can provide an extra accent of light that can improve the look of the talent.

Triple Key

A popular variation on traditional three-point lighting is "four-point" lighting or **triple key**. Essentially, three key lights provide forward illumi-nation on each target. One key light is positioned 45 degrees up, out, and to the left (exactly like a traditional key). The next key light is positioned 45 degrees up, out, and straight at dead center or 90 degrees head-on. The final key light is positioned 45 degrees up, out, and to the right (exactly like a traditional fill). All three instruments are matched (typically 1K fresnels or LED equivalents). The lights in the traditional key and fill posi-tions are aimed and tuned the same as in traditional three point. The new "center" key is aimed at the nose, and defocused to the same level as the others. A back light is added in the manner described above. Hair lights, kickers, and side lights may be added if desired.

FLOOD LIGHTING

The next lighting strategy is quick, efficient, and highly flexible. However, the use of a ring of flood lights to illuminate a news set is not rocket sci-ence. And, the "look" that is achieved may not be as appealing as the three-point strategy, as it is much "flatter" in character.

To begin the process, imagine a circle on the studio floor that encom-passes the news set. From that imaginary circle on the floor, extrapolate the circle to the lighting grid at a 45-degree angle. The general placements of the lighting instruments will be along the imaginary line created on the grid.

The areas of placement that will need the most attention will be the front of the circle (functioning as the key lights for the talent) and the rear of the circle (the back lights). Although halogen softboxes are often used in a bank strategy, LED panels have some advantages (quality of the light, heat, electric consumption, etc.). Whatever specific instrument is selected, take care not to mix different bulb types.

LED softboxes/panels can be mounted on the grid at 45 degrees. LEDs are aimed in the same fashion as the fluorescents.

The lights along the rear of the circle are basically functioning as back-lights and/or **kickers**. Again, softboxes (halogen) or panels (LED) or other flood lighting may be used, but the ideal is to match the instruments used in the front to offer a similar quality of light across the entire set. Mount a row that covers the width of the set and yet high enough to avoid an unwanted cameo. At this point, additional lighting "banks" can be added to the left and right portions of the layout circle if so desired.

LIGHTING A CHROMA KEY WALL

The chroma key wall must be lit evenly for the key effect to work well. Newer technology (such as traditional ultimatte keyers – embedded in Grass Valley switchers) in keying is much more forgiving, but nonetheless a smooth lighting job will make the weather forecast (or any other use of the chroma key set-up appear clean.

Begin by lighting the chroma key wall with either LED panels, grid-mounted cyc lights (ideal – ground rows will also work), or halogen soft-boxes. The downward wash effect should be such that nearly all of the light is on the chroma key wall or cyc and is well contained in the immediate floor area where the two meet. The light should be even, smooth, and not so intense as to make the wall appear white (color is key).

One technique to light the area where the weather anchor will deliver the forecast is to begin by marking a parallel line to the cyc or wall about 4 to 5 feet out from the wall. The line should extend the entire width of the chroma key wall or cyc that will be in use. The weather anchor will walk back and forth along this line and needs to be well lit at all points along it.

From a centered, standing position, hold both arms straight out from your body. Move them up to the grid at a 45-degree angle. Now, begin to separate your arms to about 55 degrees – the spots you are pointing to mark the light placements. Hang low wattage fresnels with diffusion in each position (or diffused broads with barndoors). Defocus each (fully flood) in order to permit the entire line of action to be covered. Use the barndoors to sharply control any spill on the chroma key wall.

Each of these lights really functions like fill lights and a key will need to be added. The key in this situation will need to be head on (90 degrees) and at a steep enough angle so as to not interfere with (throw a shadow on) the chroma key wall. The choice of light is crucial. A good technique is to use a small, highly diffused broad with barndoors or a small panel as the key. Lighting a chroma key wall is 50 percent art and 50 percent science and experimentation will be required to get the best result for your particular set-up. A good rule of thumb is that separation is of the upmost importance, both physically and electronically. The subject needs to be far enough from the wall to be lit "separately" (and to minimize the color spilling from the wall back onto the subject.

Effects Lighting

After lighting the talent, any other lighting is lighting for effect. Common lights will illuminate the flat wall or background curtain (cyc lights and grid-mounted softboxes are good choices). Ellipsoidals can be used to accent the front of the news desk or project a station logo. Take care not to over-light your set – the use of too many effects lights will distract from the content of the news program and may suggest more of a game show feel to your viewers. "Add more lasers!"

5

STUDIO CAMERAS AND FLOOR DIRECTING

INTRODUCTION

The following chapter describes three common technical production assignments in the studio. The jobs are fairly straightforward. The **Studio Camera Operator** refers to the person assigned to operate any given studio television camera. In many studios, each camera will have an operator. However, a definite trend in studio-based camera work is the appearance of robotic and remote-controlled cameras. Not all studios, therefore, will hire a camera operator for each camera. Often, one person can control all of the camera units with a joy-stick and a computer.

The **Floor Director** is the technical "boss" of the studio, and the best Floor Directors are knowledgeable about all of the other technical jobs in the studio so that they may assist others if needed. The Floor Director's primary job is to communicate with the talent. And, the Floor Director operates/functions as the eyes, ears, and mouth of the Director to some extent. Studio safety can be another responsibility of the Floor Director. When a show is live, or is in production, the Floor Director is the ultimate authority in the studio.

STUDIO CAMERA

A person assigned to the Studio Camera position is responsible for operating the studio camera unit. The usual protocol during production is to refer to the position by camera number, rather than operator name, so the camera number becomes a proper name of sorts. "Camera One, come help me coil this cable."

The job begins before the show starts. The operator will need to deploy the camera first. Preparing to move a camera and rolling a camera across a studio floor is not as simple as it may appear. Pedestal-mounted camera

DOI: 10.4324/9780429244100-5

units are heavy, tethered to the control room through a patch panel via a thick **camera cable**, **locked** into position with at least five separate locking mechanisms, and are expensive (30 thousand dollars per unit is "average").

If the camera unit is "parked" along the studio wall (as they often are), the operator will need to "unlock" the wheels first (three wheels, three locks). The **wheel lock** prevents the wheel from moving. On some units, wheel locks are sistered with directional locks that "lock" the wheels in a particular direction or plane.

Unlock the wheels, taking care not to lock the wheels in a particular direction, and move the camera away from its parking spot, taking care not to put undue stress on the camera cable. Camera cables are commonly spooled like a garden hose on the studio wall or figure-eight wrapped on the studio floor.

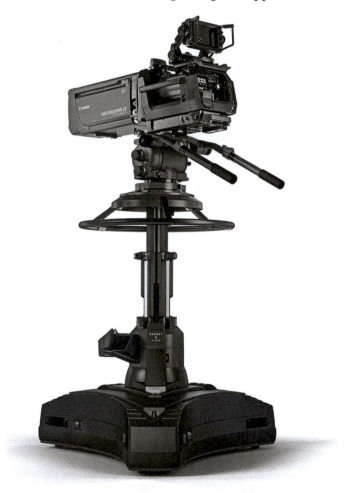

Figure 5.1 Studio Camera Unit – Osprey Studio S Pedestal

(Courtesy Videndum Production Solutions, Inc.)

Drive Safe

Often, it is good form to have one person deal with the cable while another person "drives" the camera to position. The appropriate spot to grab, push, and steer the camera is the **"pedestal steering wheel."**

While "driving" a camera, take care not to run over any cables, equipment, or people. Drive slowly – it is possible to "wreck" a camera just like one "wrecks" a car. Once the camera is in position, the camera operator will need to unlock the rest of the camera unit and begin a sequence of tasks to power-up and tune the camera.

UNLOCK THE LOCKS

Just about all studio camera units will have a **pedestal** or **column lock** that prevents the camera from moving up and down. The lock may be colored "red" or labeled in some other fashion, but once it is located, it will need to be released. If the lock is a "knob" of some kind, it can be released by rotating it counter-clockwise (thus to engage the lock, rotate clockwise). As the column mechanism may be under pressure, care should be exercised when initially disengaging this type of lock.

If the lock is a ring or tab-type lock, you will need to push down on the camera unit, turn the ring or lift up on the tab, and release the unit. A word of caution – some camera units have both types of locks. The pedestal or column lock is released when the operator can move the entire camera unit up and down freely and smoothly. The camera should be positioned at a comfortable height for the operator as well as provide an eye level view of the talent.

On the pedestal head, two more locks are standard – the **tilt lock** and the **pan lock**. Again, the manufacturer may have color-coded the locks to ease identification, but they must be located and disengaged before the unit can be used properly. The tilt lock and pan lock are usually knob-type locks but vary by manufacturer (some look like levers) – to disengage the locks, rotate the knob (or lever) counterclockwise.

The pan lock has been released when the camera pivots freely from left to right. The tilt lock has been released when the camera pivots freely to "look" up or "look" down. One more lock may be present – the **master lock**. Not all units will have it. If the operator has released the tilt lock and the unit will not pivot, a master lock is present. Usually it is a large, spring-loaded pin that is located "through" the pedestal head. In order to release it, locate the "head" of the pin, pull it out from the head and twist it so that it will "hold" open. The camera should now "tilt" freely. (To re-lock a master lock of this type, turn the head of the pin and allow the pin to "slip" back through the head – (careful – this one is a common finger-eater).

The camera unit is fully unlocked when it can roll in any direction, move up and down, pivot left and right, and pivot up and down. The protocol for any given studio will vary, but it is good form to re-engage the tilt lock when leaving the camera unattended (even for a moment) while it is deployed.

PARTS AND PIECES

The Viewfinder

The **viewfinder** on the camera "shows" the operator what the camera "sees." When the camera is powered-up, the viewfinder will also be receiving power (there is usually no on/off switch). However, it is common to turn the brightness and/or contrast controls down to prevent the LCD panel from burning-in an image and/or from wearing out prematurely.

The camera operator will need to adjust the viewfinder image (brightness/contrast) and the viewfinder position (it pivots and tilts). Located on the front of the viewfinder will be a **tally light**. When the tally light is "on," it means that the camera is selected to video program – the camera is hot, active, or live (the one everyone is looking at). On a side note, tally lights can usually be turned off at the viewfinder as well.

The viewfinder can also be used to monitor either one or two channels of **return video**. Typically, in a one-channel system, program video is routed as return video. In a two-channel system, the second channel of return video can be used to monitor preview or to view the output of a second Mix Effects Bus – thus the camera operator can frame a shot for a specific look. Return buttons are located either on top of or underneath of the servo zoom control (mounted on the right "stick" or handlebar.

Camera Control Unit (CCU) and Power

The camera unit is operated both manually and by remote control (not to be confused with a robotic pedestal). The remote control for the camera is called the **Camera Control Unit (CCU)**. The CCU is commonly located in the control room and is operated and tuned by a Broadcast Engineer.

The camera is usually powered by remote (as opposed to battery power or an independent AC/DC unit). However, the operator in the studio may need to "tell the camera" how it is to be powered. The power indicator switch will need to be properly set to CCU and the power switch will need to be set to the "on" position.

It is important to note that specific studio cameras will vary widely by manufacturer. Each studio will be slightly different in its camera configuration and the protocols for powering up a camera unit will also vary. Once the camera is powered up, the internal imaging chips – **complementary metal-oxide semiconductors (CMOSs)** – will need to be tuned and balanced with the other cameras through the CCUs. The Broadcast Engineer will **white-balance** the cameras and adjust how the cameras "see" specific colors and "view" contrast.

Prompter Power and Input

The teleprompter equipment mounted on the front of the camera unit will need to be powered up (if so-equipped). A separate on/off switch (apart from the camera) may be located on the prompter unit. However, some prompter units will simply draw power from the same source as the camera (if the camera is on the prompter is on).

Like any video monitor, the prompter unit may be able to monitor multiple video inputs. Therefore, the camera operator will need to ensure the unit is switched to the appropriate input (typically, the teleprompter output *or* video program for the weather section of the show).

INTERCOM

Headset, Belt Pack, XLR Cable

Once the camera is ready to go, the camera operator will need to locate an **intercom unit** in order to communicate with the control room and the rest of the production crew. The intercom unit is either built into the camera or is separately connected to the system. The basic "wired" intercom unit has three parts: the **headset**, the **beltpack**, and an **XLR cable** of some length that will hook into the patch panel.

The "wireless" version has the headset and a beltpack that has a built-in wireless receiver/transmitter.

It is common to operate a two-channel intercom system (sometimes called the PL, *party-line*) so that the Director can isolate certain crew members on a particular channel. The camera operator will need to know what channel(s) to monitor on the intercom and make volume adjustments for the headphone portion of the headset – both controls are located on the beltpack (or on the camera body itself).

The final control on the beltpack controls the microphone of the headset. Usually, a button can be pressed to activate the microphone. When the button is released, the microphone will go dead. To keep the microphone active (on some beltpacks), press the button twice (quickly) and the microphone should stay "on." Similar microphone controls (often a

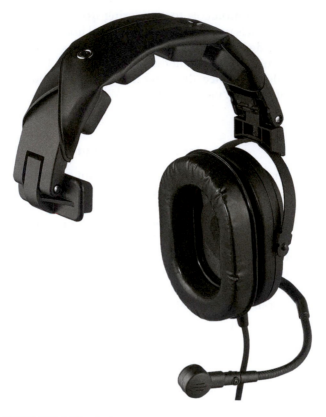

Figure 5.2 RTS™ HR-1 Headset
(Courtesy Telex)

three-position toggle-type switch) are located on the rear of the camera body if the beltpack is built-in.

CAMERA OPERATIONS

Set the Drag/Friction Controls

Located near to the pan lock and tilt lock on most professional pedestals the camera operator will find controls for **pan drag/friction** and **tilt drag/ friction**. **Drag or Friction** is the relative resistance the pedestal head will give when a camera operator attempts to pan, or alternately, attempts to tilt.

The correct adjustment for drag depends on the weight of the camera, the type of pedestal head, and the preference of the operator. A correctly adjusted set-up will permit the camera operator to make camera moves very, very smoothly.

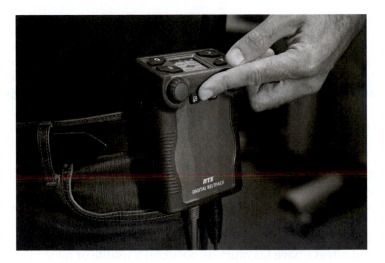

Figure 5.2a Close-ups of RTS™ DBP intercom beltpack
(Courtesy Telex)

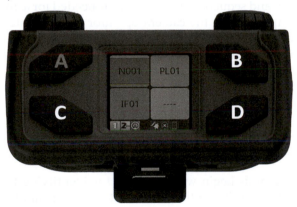

Figure 5.2b Close-ups of RTS™ DBP intercom beltpack

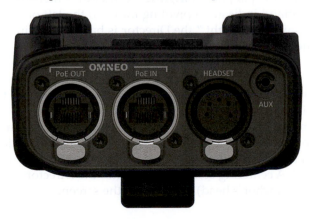

Figure 5.2c Close-ups of RTS™ DBP intercom beltpack

Set-Focus

At the point that production commences, the camera operator will need to anticipate and respond to commands from the Director. However, certain operations will need to be performed without a specific direction to do so. For example, the camera operator will need to "**set focus**." To do this, the camera operator will need to zoom in as far as possible to the target (usually an anchor's eye – it has a lot of detail). The camera operator will then need to adjust the focus control to get the most crisp image possible (if the anchor is not available, try the edge of the anchor's chair).

Once the focus is "set," the camera operator can zoom out to the **framing** appropriate for the needs of the program. As long as the camera does not move toward or away from the target (or as long as the target does not move), the focus should remain correct through the range of the zoom. The camera operator is an image provider and creator – the camera operator should always have (as much as possible) a usable or needed shot for the Director to select from.

The camera operator may use a **shot sheet** (a list of shots) as a reminder of the progression and sequence of compositions needed for a given program. Again, it is important for the camera operator to anticipate the Director, not merely react to directing commands. When a Director does give a command to a camera operator, the camera operator should comply as quickly and as smoothly as possible – the camera operator also needs to know (at all times) if the camera they are operating is the active program source.

CAMERA COMMANDS

Pan, Tilt, Dolly, Truck

Common commands begin with the Director identifying the camera by number and then specifying the desired action. For example, the Director might say "camera one, set focus and re-set your shot." Other common commands include: pan, tilt, dolly, truck, center or center-up, and zoom.

A **pan** command indicates a pivoting move to the left or to the right; if the Director says, "pan right," the Director is basically saying, "show me what is to the right." A **tilt** command is also a pivoting move – either "up" or "down."

To **dolly** is to move the entire camera unit forward or backward. "Camera One, dolly-in" or "dolly-out," as the case may be. A **truck** command is an indication to move the entire unit left or right.

During any move, the camera operator should maintain a consistent and average speed. Do not halt a move until the Director indicates – you don't want a Director saying, "Camera One, pan right," then "a little more … a bit more." A centering command indicates the Director wants the target (maybe the anchor's head) centered on the screen.

Zoom

Zoom commands indicate the desire to "zoom in" or "zoom out" as the case may be. To activate a zoom, locate the zoom control. The zoom control is a thumb lever that you press to the right (zoom in) or to the left (zoom out). Although newer zoom controllers have speed dials that can be preset, operators should be aware that many zoom controllers are pressure sensitive – the harder you hit it, the faster the zoom.

CAMERA TIPS

The requirements of the camera operator position are different for every show, every director, and will vary from studio to studio. The camera operator will need to become highly proficient in the use of the studio camera in order to be of value to the Director. The operator will need to be flexible – able to capture/acquire professional quality images while responding to the technical requirements of the camera itself.

A few tips are warranted: anticipate the Director (stay one step ahead of what the Director will need); begin and end each camera move with a decent composition (start a move on a good shot and end on a well-composed shot); be consistent and be smooth (the speed of a zoom or the speed of a move should be consistent from beginning to end); the Director should never have to issue a command twice (listen well); and, never use the intercom system as your own personal walkie-talkie (not only is it really poor form to chat on the intercom, when the Director speaks, the crew listens).

When the program is completed, the camera operator is responsible for striking the camera unit. The unit will need to be powered down, the viewfinder dimmed if need be, the camera cable will need to be re-coiled or wrapped, the camera will need to be re-parked and entirely locked down. Finally, the intercom unit will need to be properly stowed.

Composition Tips

Headroom

Headroom is the visual distance from the top of the talent's head to the top edge of the video monitor. Too much headroom means that, visually, there is too much space between the talent's head and the top of the picture. Although it is uncommon, it is possible to have too little headroom. The choice is an artistic one that will need to be negotiated between the Director and the Camera Operator.

Leadroom

Leadroom is the visual distance that is to the front of a moving object (like a car passing by) or to the front of a visual composition of a person's head. If the talent on camera is looking to the right or to the left, "room to look into" should be provided.

CAMERA MOUNTS AND ALTERNATIVES

A very wide array of **camera mounts** are available. Common alternatives to the studio pedestal include:

Cranes and Jibs

A crane or **jib** mount (the terms really are used as synonyms) is an arm that pivots on a fixed point – typically a tripod or pedestal (with dollies). The length of the arm is highly variable (6ft to 40 ft). On one end of the arm, the camera is mounted. On the other end of the arm, counterweights are fixed to allow for the entire unit to move with ease.

Gimbals and Steadicams

A gimbal is a stabilizing camera mount that keeps a camera level as a camera is moved. A gimbal will keep a camera unit level on the horizontal axis and plumb on the vertical axis. Gimbals are commonly used for cameras that are handheld in POV shots or other shots where the camera is moving or "following" a subject. Gimbals can be mounted to cranes/jibs or on any type of grip or handle (common with video blogging).

Steadicam is a trademark of the Tiffen company. A Steadicam is a type of larger and more complex camera gimbal that is "worn" by the camera operator (typically in a vest design). A steadicam includes a platform for the camera (often called the "sled"), a tripod-like head is usually beneath that, an external monitor mount, and batteries to run the whole set-up. The function of a steadicam is the same as a gimbal.

Rigs, Sliders, Dollies

A camera rig is any type of "shouldered" camera mount that allows for greater control of "handheld" shots. Typically included with a rig will be a camera mount of some kind (often called a "cage"), a shoulder plate (some are single some are double, and handlebars of some type that allow for the camera operator to hang-on to the whole thing.

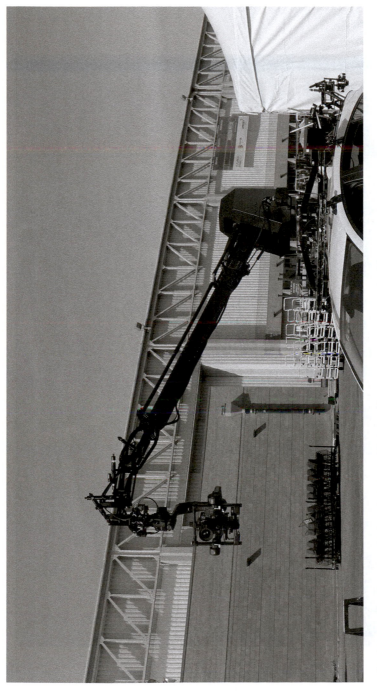

Figure 5.3 Crane/Jib Mount with Gimbal (car roof mount)

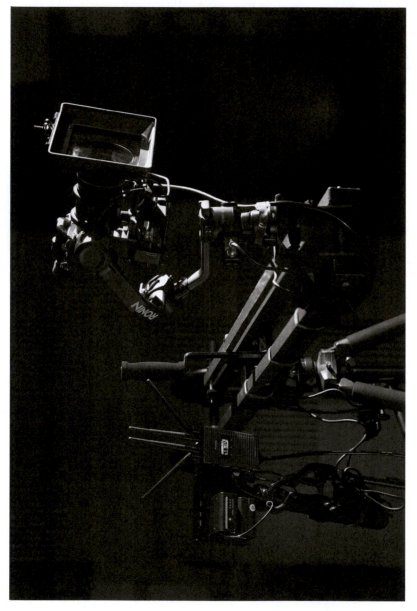

Figure 5.3a ProAM USA Taurus Jr. HD60 Crane/Jib Mount with Gimbal
(Courtesy ProAm USA)

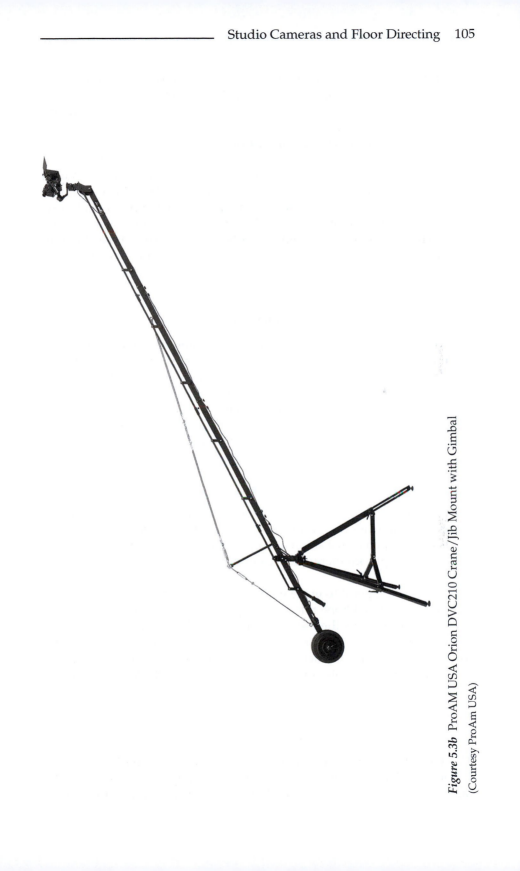

Figure 5.3b ProAM USA Orion DVC210 Crane/Jib Mount with Gimbal
(Courtesy ProAm USA)

A slider is a camera mount that allows for (you guessed it) ... the camera to slide along a fairly short and fixed track. Some sliders are manual (the operator has to "push" the camera along the track) and some are mechanized in such a way that a small electric motor will move the camera back-and-forth along the track using a controller.

Dollies are larger camera mounts that are basically flat platforms with four wheels. A few types of these are large enough to accommodate the camera operator (a dolly with a seat). The dolly can be pushed or pulled on just about any smooth surface. And yet another type of dolly uses "dolly tracks" for the platforms to allow for super smooth camera movement. The nice thing about dolly tracks is that many tripods can be fitted with the wheels that will ride on the tracks (so a separate platform would not be needed in that set-up).

Cable Cams

One of the newest and most popular camera mounts is the cable cam. A cable cam set-up uses one or two (parallel) cables that span (typically) over an athletic playing field or any other open air space above a subject (perhaps over an audience at a concert venue or over the stage). The mount is usually a single wheel that rides on top of a single cable or a small platform (wheels on both sides) with gimbal set-ups for the cameras. The video signal travels by fiber optic back to the switcher.

Drones

Aerial video is another recent (and now common) development in the industry. What was once the fairly rare realm of helicopter and fixed wing pilots is now open to just about anyone willing to learn how to fly a drone. A drone is simply another type of camera mount in the applications of the industry.

An interesting point to make with drones is that most are used in violation of FAA policy. Drone pilots are required (in the USA) to be licensed. FAA part 107 governs the use of drones under 55 pounds. A small carve-out in the law allows for flying under an exception for recreation ("flying for fun or personal enjoyment"). However, if you intend to fly a drone to shoot video or take photographs, assume that you will need to be certified under FAA Part 107.

Floor Directing

The **Floor Director** is the senior production staff position in the studio. While the Floor Director's primary responsibility is to work with the talent, the job often requires rendering assistance to camera operators,

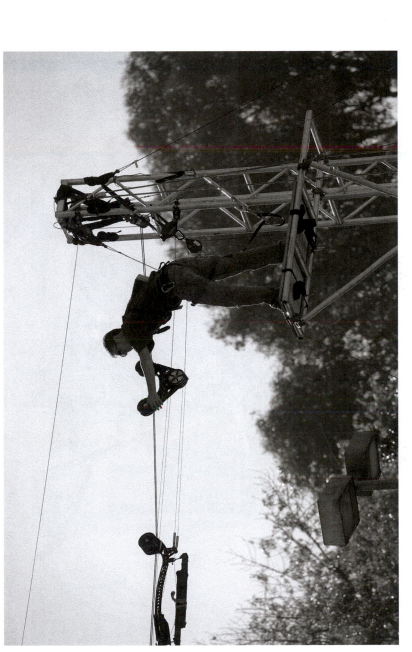

Figure 5.4 Rigging a Cable Cam; Los Angeles Memorial Coliseum: Production crew on the set of ESPN College GameDay built by The Home Depot

(Photo by Allen Kee/courtesy ESPN Images)

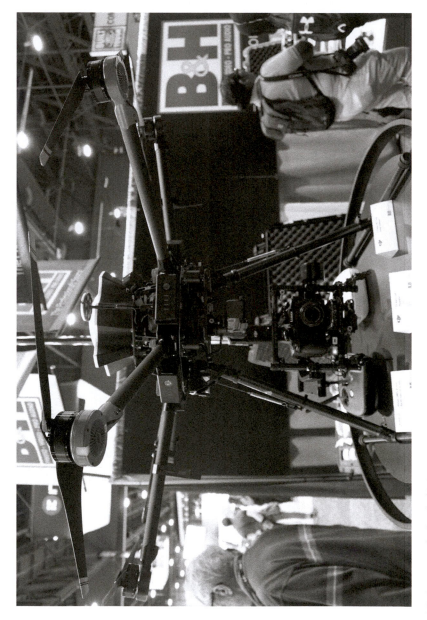

Figure 5.5 DJI Drone with Gimbal Mount

gaffers, audio technicians, and others who work in the studio environment. The more effective Floor Directors to work with, it follows, are ones that have "worked their way up" through the other studio positions first.

A Floor Director is like an in-studio representative of the Director. The Floor Director relays commands from the Director to the entire studio staff – some of these will be audible, some will be "translated" to hand gestures. The Floor Director is also responsible for communicating with the anchors on set – for cuing the anchors – and for assisting the anchors with the technical requirements of the television studio. The Floor Director is also responsible for "hosting" any guests in the studio that may be a part of a given program. As host, the Floor Director is responsible for escorting the guest to the set, seating the guest, mounting/dressing a microphone for the guest, and ushering them out of the studio. (Be prepared to be a guest gopher – "… water please," "… why certainly Mr. Pawlowski").

The Floor Director in Preproduction

Prior to the beginning of the program, the Floor Director will review the rundown of the show (an outline of the events of the program) in order to identify any major technical changes that have been planned for that particular broadcast. Television programs follow fairly specific technical recipes in order to reduce confusion among the production crew. For example, the newscast may "always" begin with a dollying reverse-zoom on Camera 2 and a dissolve to Camera 1 for the introduction of the first story. Another example might concern the operations in playback – "always" beginning with DDR A at the top of a block.

Any major changes to the rundown will need to be identified and sorted out among the production crew. The Floor Director will take the lead on communicating these changes to the studio staff – including the anchors.

Prior to the show, the Floor Director will need to prepare an intercom set-up (as described above) in order to communicate with the control room and the rest of the production crew. The Floor Director will pre-check to be sure the lighting grid is powered-up properly (and may assist a Lighting Director in changing out bulbs if needed). And, although many anchors prefer to "dress" their own microphones, it is not uncommon (and is sometimes expected) that the Floor Director will assist with this task as well.

Safety issues are also an important part of the Floor Director's job. For example, monitors on wheels need to be placed where they can be seen by all, but the cabling will need to be "dressed" so that the wires cannot be run over by the cameras, tripped over by the talent or the guests, etc.

FLOOR DIRECTING THE STUDIO STAFF

Communicate

Once the talent is miked, seated, and the mic checks have been completed, it is good form for the talent to remain in position for the rest of the program. Therefore, it is not uncommon for the talent to request water (or other items) from the Floor Director. While this "gophering" is usually not a problem in a professional environment, talent should be careful not to abuse the privilege, and, Floor Directors should take care not to encourage the behavior.

Once the talent is in position on the set, the Floor Director should be sure to discuss any technical changes in the rundown or other blocking

The Floor Director and the Director

Responding to Time Cues

Floor Director will speak	Floor Director will show
"one minute"	one finger
"30 seconds"	crossed arms or C shaped hand
"15 seconds"	fist
"stand-by"	full hand, palm out, fingers up

Responding to commands from the Director

Floor Director hears	Floor Director will
cue	swing from "stand by" downward toward the talent
wrap	hand/ fist/ finger "rotates" in the air
cut	finger "cuts" across neck
stretch	hands "pull" imaginary taffy
ready to swing	arms out with both hands "pointing" at active camera
swing	both hands "sweep" toward incoming camera
take	arms out, both hands "pointing" at new active camera

Figure 5.6 Description of common Floor Director hand signals

changes that are planned with the entire studio staff. The communication between the Floor Director and the anchors needs to be effective. Have you ever seen an anchor looking at the wrong camera? Well, the person responsible was more than likely the Floor Director.

In any production situation, the communication protocols between the Floor Director and the talent must be worked out in advance. The Floor Director, to some extent, helps to make the anchors look good. By filtering and translating the headset chatter, the Floor Director keeps the communication in the studio efficient, calm, and on point.

Cuing Talent, Cuing the Studio Crew

The cues that a Floor Director gives will either be audible "echoes" of the Director or Assistant Director or "translated" into silent hand signals/ gestures. The choice of cue is determined by the conditions of the microphones – if the mics are hot the cues will be silent – if the mics are off the cues can be audible.

Cues need to be easily seen and/or heard by the crew, given quickly and efficiently, and must not interfere with the production. There is no need, then, to give cues while crouching in the front of a camera. The Floor Director should stand to the side of the active camera (the camera in program) or next to the immediate following camera (the camera in preview).

The hands of the Floor Director should never pass in front of the camera lens nor should cues be given forward of the lens itself (this includes "below" the lens cues). Generally, cues are fairly standardized in the industry; and, the cues described in Figure 5.6 are some of the more common you may encounter.

6

NEWSROOM COMPUTER SYSTEMS, PROMPTER, GRAPHICS, PLAYBACK, REMOTES, ENGINEERING

INTRODUCTION

The following chapter describes crew positions that are usually located in the control room. The jobs are structured by the particular hardware and software installation – the equipment package – to be found in a given television station. For example, the procedures associated with the Graphics position will vary a great deal depending on the hardware/software package used to create, store, manage, and recall the graphics. Nonetheless, certain common tasks and procedures are associated with these jobs.

This chapter also describes two fairly common special effects – digital video effects (DVE) and keying. Again, depending on how the control room is set-up, these tasks can be handled by the Technical Director and/or the Graphics position. The use of image store (aka electronic still-store – ESS) in the newscast is another procedure that fits here. It is important to remember that much of what this chapter will cover can and will vary depending on the hardware and/or software that has been purchased and installed. As such, some of these jobs have become rather proprietary or specialized.

Newsroom Computer Systems

At this point, it is important to introduce the idea of Newsroom Computer Systems (NCS or NRCS). In the mid-1990s, it became apparent that the integration of production components from many separate manufacturers was, essentially, a non-starter.

DOI: 10.4324/9780429244100-6

At the time, prompter systems, video editing systems, audio and video servers, graphics systems, playback servers, and content organization software could not "talk" to each other very well (unless those systems happened to be "integrated" products from the same manufacturer). And, even though a very few manufacturers had created limited "suites" of hardware/software that were integrated and worked well together, few television operations were willing to invest in these narrow proprietary systems without assurances that a machine from company "A" would work well with a machine from company "B" and so on.

So, without an agreement in place for a basic communication command structure, machines from separate manufacturers simply would not "play well" with one another without a common language or file protocol in place. Thus, to integrate the newsroom (and the control room), all of the separate manufacturers had to come together and agree upon a basic communication protocol. The MOS project is the result of these agreements. FYI: the MOS project began as an initiative of the Associated Press.

MOS (in this usage) stands for media object server. The MOS is a communication command structure (a protocol) that essentially uses "file pointers" to allow each machine on a given network to "find" a media asset (typically on a central server). And, each machine on the network can use the same asset at the same time (for example, a machine does not have to "wait in line" to use a particular audio file). Now, a media asset can be just about any type of file (video, audio, graphics, script, still-image, rundown, CG) created by just about any type of machine. All files will integrate as long as the files are MOS-based.

The use of a basic, top-level organizing software imposes structure on all of this in the forms required for the production of a program (a playlist of pre-recorded clips for playback, a rundown for the producers that is a "living" document (with the ability to integrate changes on the fly), playlists for graphics, etc.). The top-level organizing software is called the Newsroom Computer System (NRCS). Although NRCS stands for Newsroom Computer System, do not be surprised to find the software used for the production of other types of programming (interview shows, game shows, reality shows, etc.). Note: perhaps a better name for the software would be PCS – Production Control System … just my two cents.

As it stands, three NRCS software packages dominate the North American and Western European market:

- The Associated Press' ENPS (electronic news production system)
- AVID's MediaCentral / Cloud UX (united experience)
- Octopus.

However, a few other NRCS software packages are available:

- Ross' Inception News
- Annova OpenMedia.

PROMPTER

The **teleprompter** is a computer that turns a script into a scrollable graphic. Once the script is in this graphic form, it is transmitted as video to a monitor (typically an LCD panel) mounted horizontally off of the front of the studio camera units. The image from the monitor is projected onto a one-way mirror mounted diagonally in front of the camera lens. The camera lens is covered in a fabric tent to limit light flow from behind the mirror – increasing the contrast of the projected image.

As anchors look at the camera, then, they do not see the lens of the camera, rather a flat glass mirror that is reflecting an image of the script. Prompter units are after-market camera accessories – they are purchased as add-ons to the camera units from manufacturers who specialize in these packages. One popular system to explore is CueScript.

The prompter computer can be any PC that runs the operating system required by the software manufacturer. Teleprompting software usually operates like an extraordinarily basic word processing package; and the software may be tied into newsroom management software (like the ENPS package from the Associated Press).

Prompters tend to operate in two modes: **edit mode** and **prompt mode**. In edit mode, scripts can be loaded manually, imported as files, saved, and edited – basically treated like any other word processing document. In prompt mode, the script becomes a scrollable graphic. Often the control mechanism for the scroll can be handled with a mouse wheel or by using the scroll bar associated with the document window. Other controls will be located in dropdown menus as associated with the software. This might include the usual document formatting controls like color, font, size, alignment, underline, bold, and line spacing but may also control scroll speeds and other prompting functions.

Prompter Crew Position

The person who operates the teleprompter computer is usually referred to as "Prompter." The job may be filled by a member of the production crew if the job only requires script recall, but it is not uncommon to find a member of the producing staff in the position (a writer). Again, if the job merely requires script recall, a production crew member can easily fulfill the requirement.

However, in a breaking news situation, or in a larger metropolitan news market, the job may be best left to a writer – or other member of the producing staff. With some integrated software packages, changes can be made to the script from any networked PC after the show has commenced and the prompting function is engaged. All content is typically controlled by the rundown as driven by the NRCS. Prompter, playback

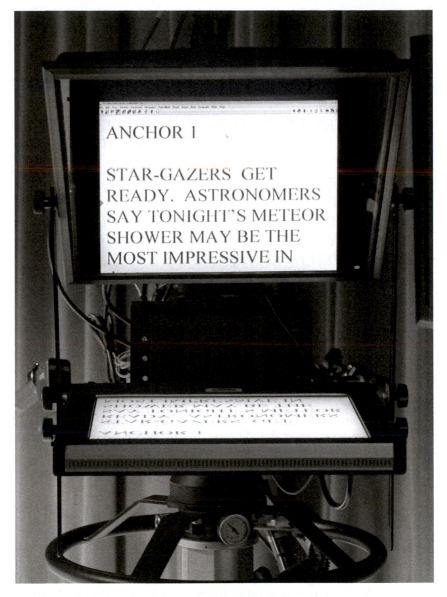

Figure 6.1 Camera Mounted Prompter Unit Display

of pre-recorded video clips, and graphic insertions are all ordered and re-ordered constantly by the rundown/NRCS.

Thus, a producer can delete and/or add script on the fly. The only requirement for operating the prompting computer in recall mode is for the operator to carefully listen to the anchors. The speed of the scroll is

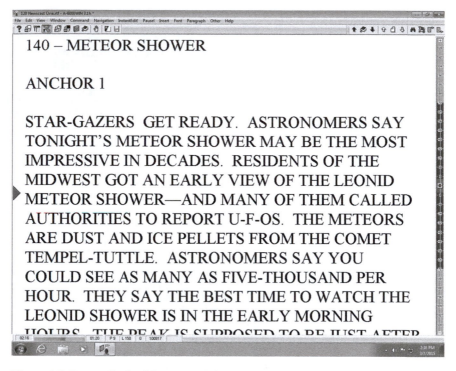

Figure 6.2 Screen Grab of Prompter PC

never consistent – one cannot "set it and forget it." The scroll speed will need to be constantly modulated based on the speech pacing of the talent.

GRAPHICS OVERVIEW

The **Graphics** operator for a typical newscast is usually located in the control room and is often simply named "Graphics" although this protocol may vary. The person(s) assigned to Graphics operate one or more computers that create and manage the files needed for two traditional functions: **character generation (CG)** and image store (**electronic still-store or ESS)**. In many cases, other functions will be added to the graphics load – 2D animations, 3D animations, 3D modeling, etc.

Character generation is the creation of text that can be keyed (layered over) another video source (like a camera shot or a video clip); or, the creation and combination of text and background that can be taken as a straight video source (like a full-screen display of sports scores or other "list of text" – election returns, etc.).

Image store (electronic still-store) is the creation and management of still-images, graphics, and illustrations that can be manipulated and keyed

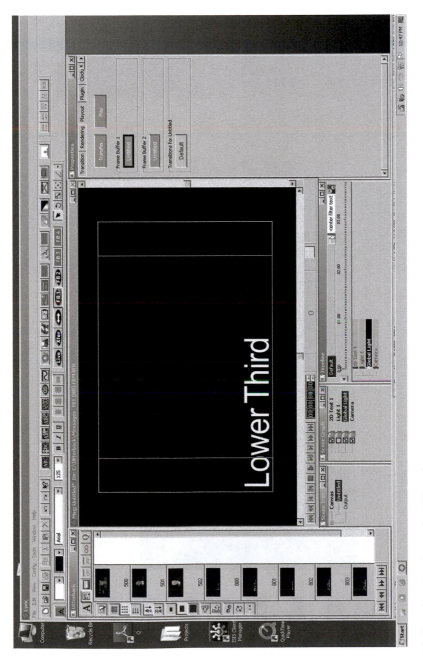

Figure 6.3 Graphics Computer in CG mode

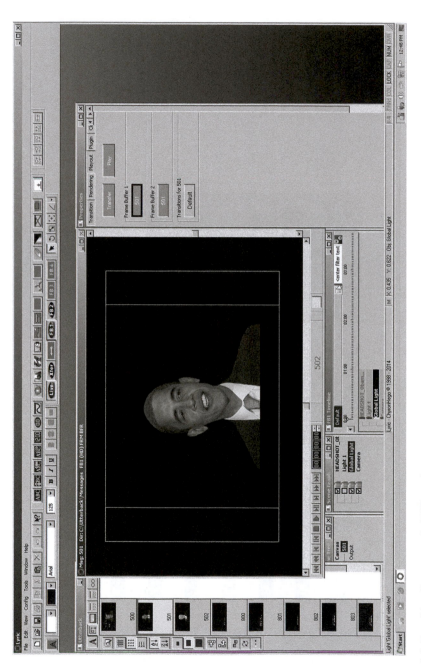

Figure 6.4 Graphics Computer in ESS mode

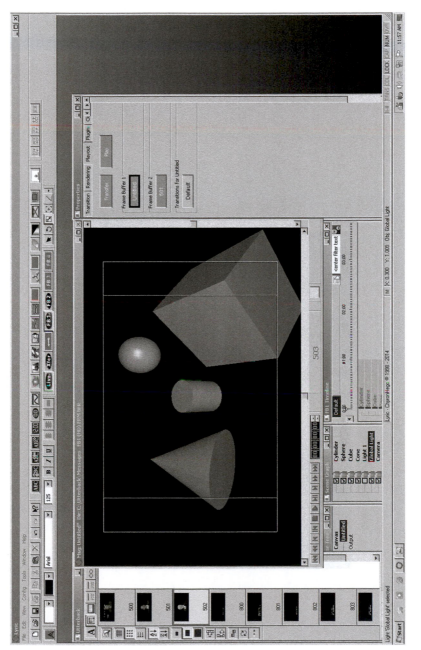

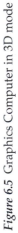

Figure 6.5 Graphics Computer in 3D mode

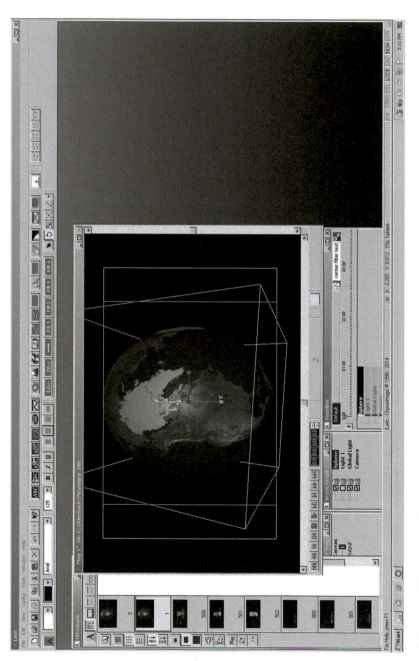

Figure 6.6 Graphics Computer in 3D mode with surface texture

(layered over other video) or can also be taken as a straight video source. Remember that in addition to the graphics computer, many video switchers have image store capability. Thus, both the switcher and the graphics computer are potential image sources.

As you might imagine, CG and image store can be combined to create multi-layered graphics that can then be saved as an entirely new and singular graphic file – (imagine a picture of Death Valley with the words "Death Valley" typed over the image). Now, you might also imagine that either element (the CG or the ESS) might be animated in some way – (the words "Death Valley" might fly onto the screen or we might start with a close-up of a cactus and zoom out to reveal a wide-shot of the valley floor). Or, both items, the CG and the ESS may animate at the same time. The animations described would be characterized as 2D animations – 2D "objects" that are programmed to move.

Additionally, with the appearance of 3D modeling software in some newsrooms, a model can be created that can be (1) used alone, (2) combined with traditional ESS, (3) combined with CG, (4) animated, (5) keyed (layered over other video) or, (6) taken as straight video. It is important to note that the choice of keying (or taking the graphics computer "straight") is typically up to the Technical Director – not the Graphics person.

DIGITAL VIDEO EFFECTS (DVE)

Furthermore, another wrinkle (and layer of complexity) can be added at this point – DVE. **Digital video effects (DVE)** can be embedded video switcher functions (thus the domain of the Technical Director) or (more rarely today) external effects units (so-called effects black boxes) that are hooked into the main video switcher as a separate video source. External DVE units may be controlled either by the TD or the Graphics operator or even both positions if need be.

Historically, external DVE units, prior to the common use of the exact same embedded functions within the switcher and/or graphics hardware/software, were originally used for some very basic effects like the "anchor box" or "split screen."

KEYING

Yet another layer of complexity can be added to this chaos and has already been alluded to – the **key**. A key is a video layer. Any video source can be keyed over any other video source. A typical example of this is a character generation (a name) that is keyed over a camera shot of a person. The CG

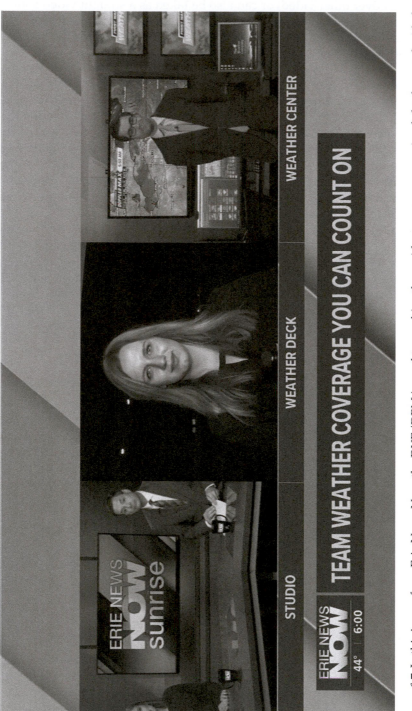

Figure 6.7 In this image from Erie News Now, the DVE/DPM is used to combine three video sources over a simple background with the addition of a keyed lower third (WICU Channel 12 and WSEE Channel 35; Erie, PA – Lilly Broadcasting)

(Courtesy Megan Solensky)

Four Different Ways to Accomplish the Same Effect

Technique One

Old School: Image Sourced from Graphics, DVE External to Switcher

The anchor box effect (where a box containing a graphic appears **over the shoulder (OTS)** of the anchor) used to be created by assigning the ESS to the DVE (which was set-up or programmed as the box shape) and then by keying (layering) the DVE over the camera. Some simple motion was possible within the DVE unit (like flying the box in or out of the frame).

Technique Two

Procedure "A": Image Sourced from Graphics, DVE Internal to Switcher

Today, the same effect can be created by keying (layering) a graphic sourced straight from the graphics computer over the camera (the DVE function – the box effect – occurs inside of the video switcher itself).

Technique Two

Procedure "B": Image Sourced from Switcher, DVE Internal to Switcher

Or, if the switcher has an internal image store (and as of this writing, most do) the same effect can be created by keying (layering) a graphic sourced from within the video switcher itself over the camera (again, the DVE function – the box effect – occurs as an internal function of the video switcher).

In both "new school" examples "A" and "B", animation functions of the DVE (movement of the box) are controlled from within the switcher using key frames and macros.

Technique Three

Procedure "C": Image Sourced from Graphics, DVE "Effect" from Graphics

The same effect can be created by keying (layering) a graphic sourced from the graphics computer over the camera. In this example, the graphics computer itself creates the "box." And, animation functions of the effect (movement of the box) are controlled from within the graphics computer using a simple program (the same as switcher key frames and macros).

To the observant, the simple conclusion is that, today, effects can be accomplished in more than one way. The capability of switchers has expanded. The capability of graphics computers has expanded.

Another Old School Effect

The split screen effect was enabled by a two-channel DVE unit where one camera signal was assigned to DVE Channel A, the other camera to DVE Channel B, and the DVE was either taken as a straight video source to Program or keyed (layered yet again) over some other video source (like a pre-set background).

Today, the same effect can be created within the switcher (in at least two different ways), using the graphics live or from internal switcher storage.

(as sourced from the graphics computer) is key – the layer. The camera image is the background.

Another typical key that is frequently used is a station or network branding "**bug**" or "watermark". The "bug" is sourced from the graphics computer and layered – "keyed" – over video program.

While this example is straightforward, consider that an animated video source (a 3D model of the Earth) can also be a key source. Imagine the Earth spinning in the center of the screen. Now consider that an animated video source (spinning Earth) can be assigned to a DVE and the DVE assigned as the key source. The DVE is programmed to "fly" from a centered infinity point forward to fill the screen. The spinning Earth starts very small in the center and grows to fill the screen (blocking out the background).

Now consider the capability of a two channel DVE – two separate animations flying independently over a background.

The final insult is the very real consideration that many switchers can handle four to six key sources at one time (five to –seven full layers of video (six key, one background) – each independently controlled) and one only begins to understand the current "look" of CNN's Headline News or a MLB game.

Types of Keys: Linear, Luminance, and Chroma

For the entry-level production technician, a basic awareness of the types of keys is important. The three most common types of keys are as follows: linear keys; luminance keys; and chromakeys. Remember that a key is a video layer. A key effect is a composite in the sense that what you see on program are essentially two video sources that have been combined. The type of key is defining how that key is electronically processed by the video switcher. The following explanations are oversimplified. For the student that wants to learn more about keying, the best explanations are typically found in the "owner's manuals" of the video switchers.

Linear Keys

A linear key uses a key source (perhaps a basic CG from the graphics computer) that is layered over a background video source (such as a camera shot). Keep in mind that just about any video source (the key layer video source) can be layered over any other type of video source (the background video source).

In a linear key set-up the video switcher keyer "cuts out" the shape of the key source from the background source and "fills" the hole in the background source with the video from the key source. The key is linear in the sense that the shape of the video signal from the key source is used to "cut" the hole in the background.

At this point, it is useful to introduce the adjustments of clip and of gain in keying. In the linear example, increasing the clip increases the "depth" of the cut into the background. If you crank the clip in a linear key set-up, you will eventually "cut out" the entire background and only see the key source video (the background video will be entirely cut out of the image). And so, the clip will need to be adjusted in such a way that only the "wanted" part of the key source video is viewable over the background.

Gain adjusts the relative strength of the key video source ("the fill") and is most noticeable on the edges of the key. If one is after a sharper edge, increasing the gain (in theory) will accomplish this effect. If one is after a softer edge, decreasing the gain will cause the edges of the "layer" to soften out.

And so, the satisfactory appearance of a key will depend on the user adjusting the clip and the gain properly.

Luminance Keys

A luminance key uses a key source that, again, is "layered" over a background source. Rather than using the "shape" of the key source to create a "hole in the background," the processing uses the brightness of the key source to create the cut. So, the brightness of the key source video and the brightness of the background video are going to be important to the success of this type of key.

Typically, this type of key works best when the key source video is high contrast (such as white lettering on a black screen). The "cut" into background video will be cleaner in this set-up. The next part of the process is to "fill" the cut with a color matte. A luminance key, then, is using three video signals to create the effect (the key source video signal, the background source video signal, and the fill source video signal – "the matte fill").

Chroma Key (Chrominance Keys)

A chroma key is a bit different in the set-ups but the layering concept is the same. In a chroma key, a camera is aimed at an evenly lit solid color background in the studio (typically a chroma key green colored cyc of one sort or another). In this common example, when the anchor stands in front of the camera, the camera is seeing the anchor standing in front of a solid green background. The video switcher in this case is going to "cut out all the green" in the video signal and replace it with another video signal (in the weather forecast section of a newscast this video source is usually a weather graphic of some type – like a map – generated by a graphics computer).

The thing that is being "cut out" in this type of key is the color green. The layer in this type of key is the anchor over the map. So … the camera video appears to be "layered" over the weather graphic.

THE JOB OF GRAPHICS

Now that you are completely confused, let us return to the job and responsibilities of the crew member assigned to Graphics. For the moment, we will discuss the character generation (CG) function in isolation from the rest of what is possible in the realm of graphics.

Character Generation

Remember that the CG (Character Generation or CapGen) function is the creation of text – text that can be layered over (keyed) other video or taken straight. The Graphics operator will need to create the program CG – graphics that will be used every time the show airs: the anchor's name (Tyler Madden – WTOV9), the credit roll (Caitlin Amato – Executive Producer), and the name of the show (ETVNews). Each of these can be saved as independent graphics files that can be recalled alone or linked together and saved in sequences of files (a playlist).

Newscasts typically have a graphics format (a "look") that specifies certain fonts, sizes, and colors. The format is contained in a series of already created templates within the graphics computer. The templates are used to create the CG for the program.

Prior to the show, the Graphics operator will be primarily concerned with creating the CG needed to cover an individual program – the CG needed just for a particular show. Most graphics operators have already created the program CG (the material used every time the show airs) and will merely need to load it into a final playlist.

The CG needed to cover an individual program, as one might imagine, will vary from show to show. Names of people, places, and reporters that appear live or in the pre-recorded video clips to be used will also need to be created, saved, and loaded to a playlist (in order). One technique (among many) to manage the process is to save CG files by run number and tag them in order (100-1, 100-2, 100-3, etc.).

Requests for special graphics will need to be processed and loaded – pages of sports scores, stock reports, maps, telephone numbers to call "for more information," and the like. It is at this point that many software packages permit animations to be linked to particular CG pages (like flipping a name on to or off of the screen).

Once the graphics are created, each page will need to be loaded (organized) into a playlist for recall during the program. The organization of the playlist is over-determined by the rundown.

If using NRCS, the graphics playlist is automatically "linked" to the rundown itself, and all of the CG graphics can be created by the producer of each story – as MOS objects.

THE JOB OF GRAPHICS II

Image Store or Electronic Still-Store

The **image store** function of the Graphics operator is to acquire, create, and manage any still images that may be needed for a particular show. The image load for a news show might include but is not limited to: pictures of reporters (on the scene or otherwise reporting remotely), a map of the State of Utah, a photo of a soccer ball, an image of the Grand Canyon, the U.S. flag, Santa Claus, attack helicopters, corporate logos, ad infinitum.

Models

With the advent of 3D modeling software, imaging software (Adobe Photoshop), and compositing/illustrating software (Adobe Illustrator, Adobe After Effects), the graphics load for a news show might include topographic maps of a coal mine, 3D models of a space craft, or a drawing of a new city plan – the list of possibilities is really endless.

In any case, each graphic can be saved independently (an individual and unique file), linked with other files in a sequence, and will need to be loaded in a playlist of some fashion for recall during the program. Again, embedded animations can be linked to individual files if so desired (a spinning 3D model of the Earth is a good example).

Combine or Divide?

The Graphics position has become so complex that many news operations have attempted to manage the process by isolating and delegating graphics functions to separate crew members. It is not uncommon to find the ESS function handled entirely by the TD and the CG function isolated to one Graphics operator (who would probably be referred to as "CG" instead).

If the ESS function is not embedded in the video switcher, both the ESS function and the CG function can be separated – handled by two separate crew members on two separate graphics computers entirely apart from the TD.

Specialists in 3D modeling, animation, and compositing are often located outside of the Control Room entirely (and would be located in the newsroom or in a graphics department) with the sole purpose to create complex graphics that can be recalled (played or activated) by a crew-member during the show. In this example, the graphics are composed (created) in the pre-production environment.

Most transitions are now animated. The 3D animations can be created by the graphics department (or a Control Room Graphics Operator). The animation is not the transition. The 3D animation is "covering" the transition (usually a cut).

To activate a transition using a 3D animation: (1) the animation is "played" over the active source on program, (2) the TD cuts to the next source "underneath" the animation.

In the case of live sports programming, multiple graphic operators may be called upon to contribute to any given show (just imagine the graphic requirements of the Super Bowl or World Cup Soccer). Once the show begins, the task of the Graphics operators is to recall the graphics in order, as needed, and on the Director's command. Not only does a Graphics operator need to be fluent in the software and creative, the job requires a great deal of skill in organization and file management.

GRAPHICS AND THE DIRECTOR

The primary relationship between the Director and a Graphics operator is concerned with the supply of a resource (a graphic) at a specific time and on command.

The language a Director will use to call on a graphic will vary depending on the type of graphic (CG, ESS, an ESS sequence, an Animation, or DVE) and the intended use – keyed or straight. Consider the following:

A Super Basic Example

The Director wishes to activate a CG (Character Generator or CapGen) layer over Program Video.
Director says: Stand-By Downstream (or Font).
The Graphics operator will have re-called the appropriate CG and it will be available in CG Program as a video resource. The CG will have been prepared prior to the show in pre-production. The Technical Director will be sure the CG is selected as the appropriate key source and be prepared to activate the key.

Director says: Downstream (or Font).
The TD will activate the key.
Director says: Ready to Lose.
The TD prepares to de-activate the key.

Director says: Lose.
The TD de-activates the key. The Graphics operator can now prepare for the next graphic.

PLAYBACK

The video clips that will be utilized during a newscast are the responsibility of many people – the shooters, reporters, and editors who create the clips – and the Playback Operator who is responsible for actually "activating" or playing them – in order, as needed, and on the Director's command. The crew member that is responsible for the video clips is called "**Playback.**"

While playback operations may be located in the Control Room, it is not uncommon for the physical space to be isolated elsewhere (as audio control often is) or connected in with Master Control in some manner. It is also important to remember that most news operations have moved to a file-based environment, where video clips are stored and will be activated from one of the following machines: a **video file server** accessed via PC (typically this is one or two of the server channels that is assigned to playback); a **clip store** internal to the **video switcher**; a DDR or rack of DDRs (such as the Black Magic Design HyperDecks).

One of the tasks associated with Playback is the actual recording of the news program. Prior to the show, then, Playback will need to remember to "**roll record**" on the show. Additionally, it will be a requirement that the Playback operator be sure to double-check that the record machine is receiving video and audio program from the studio/control room cleanly (and at the appropriate signal strength). However, it is important to note that it is not uncommon for the recording task to be delegated to Master Control.

The primary responsibility of Playback will be to locate and organize the pre-recorded video clips required for the program. If multiple playback machines are in use (or multiple server channels), the machines are typically identified by letters (A, B, C, etc.) in order to reduce possible communication confusion with the Cameras.

Playback and the Director

The Directing command for "rolling" a pre-recorded video clip is straightforward. The Director will ready the clip, "Stand-by DDR A" and then "roll" the clip, "Roll DDR A."

On the ready cue, the Playback operator needs to be sure the clip is cued-up and be poised to press/activate the "play" switch or button.

On the **roll** cue the Playback operator will press/activate the play switch or button and monitor the playback. As soon as the Director is finished with the clip – the playback machine is no longer selected to program and the audio from the clip is no longer active – the playback operator can load and cue the next clip that will be needed. Remember, the average is a clip a minute – a thirty-minute newscast = 30 separate clips.

Playback and the NRCS

NRCS playback is driven by and linked to the rundown. Pre-recorded video clips are located on a server and can be triggered in a number of ways.

1. A playout computer is a server connected pc that can be manually operated by any production staff member. A video clip can be "played" or "paused" by using a typical keyboard or touch screen interface.
2. GPI (General Purpose Interface) triggers can activate video clips from a button on the switcher or a "click" – or assigned keyboard action on the graphics computer.

LIVE SHOTS, MICROWAVE, AND SATELLITE REMOTES

Live on Location

The rather ubiquitous fact-of-life in affiliate-level news operations is the seemingly endless need to "go live" from the location of a news event – even if the news event was hours (or days) in the past.

However, the arrival of the global pandemic in the early Spring of 2020 created conditions where "remote everything" was required. Anchors and reporters were, by and large, required to work from home. The use of remote equipment skyrocketed since nearly all studios and control rooms were shuttered. One particular technology dominated during this time frame (and will continue to dominate). The technology is called **bonded cellular** (more on this in a moment).

The technical requirements for getting the audio and video signals from a remote location back to the station are getting easier – especially if the news reporting is not actually live but rather "as live." An actual live remote requires an active and real time audio and video feed from the location – this is usually accomplished via bonded cellular, microwave, and (much more rarely) satellite. A report that is filed to "look live" or is handled "as live," can be fed back to the station via the internet earlier in the news day and is an "easy and efficient" protocol. A true live feed using the internet is (as of this writing) still fairly risky. Server lag, routing problems, and dropped connections are only a few of the problems still facing straight live internet feeds (streaming).

BONDED CELLULAR

The most common method for going live from a remote location in a newscast is to use a bonded cellular unit. A bonded cellular system is made up of a video and/or audio acquisition device (camera(s) and microphone(s), etc.) connected to a "magic box" that is essentially a multi-channel cell phone – the box is called an encoder. For a moment, imagine the audio and video outputs from a camera/microphone are connected to this encoder. The encoder will then make two, four, or six parallel "calls" to a cloud-based server (the number of calls depends on the bandwidth needed). The server is connected back to the control room using a strong internet connection (by strong I mean large capacity… typically 100 megabit or higher). Once the connection back into the control room is made (through a PC), the audio and video are then routed to the audio board and the video switcher as regular sources.

To add complexity, consider that the *program outputs* of both a portable video switcher and small audio mixer can be connected in similar fashion. Now the bonded cellular unit could potentially be used for other types of live events with multiple video inputs and multiple audio inputs.

As may be self-evident, the remote user will need to be in an area with strong cell coverage for the encoder connection to work. The deployment of 5G networks will, of course, impact the ability for these encoders to transmit larger amounts of data (mid-Band 5G is the most common as of this writing – currently up to about 900 megabits per second).

MICROWAVE

Going live on location using a microwave signal used to be the most common practice for the affiliate level newscast. The process was and still is fairly straightforward. A station-owned vehicle (usually a van or truck) is equipped with a telescoping tower (a pole) that holds a microwave transmitter antenna. The audio and video signals from the microphone and camera on location are encoded and then transmitted back to the television station using microwave.

The signal is typically received in Master Control where it is then separated and routed to the Control Room as a video source for the video switcher and an audio source for the audio console. However, it is not problematic for the signal to be received directly in the Playback area and then routed – forwarded – to the video switcher and audio console. Although rare, the remote signal can be received directly into the control room and hardwired as audio and video inputs.

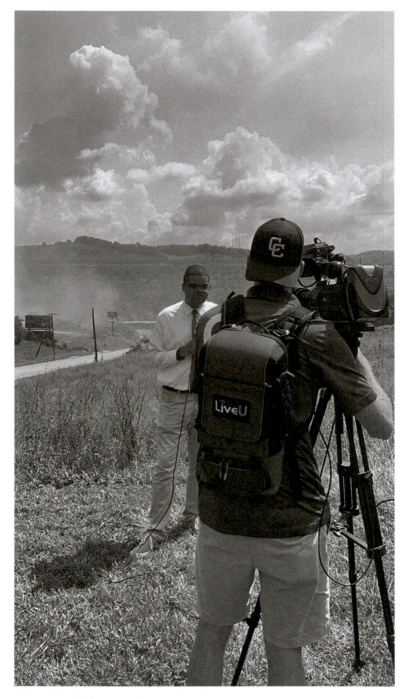

Figure 6.8 Reporter on remote; LiveU bonded cellular; WTOV Channel 9
        Steubenville, OH

(Sinclair Broadcast Group/Courtesy Tyler Madden)

The Microwave Connection

The common connection from the microwave remote vehicle is usually indirect (truck to a repeater (a relay) and then onward to the station). Since microwave hook-ups are limited as line-of-sight transmissions, repeaters are usually physically located as high as possible. Repeaters can be located on towers, mountain or hilltops, or on skyscraper roof edges (or on roof-mounted towers). The important aspect of microwave transmission to remember is that the remote truck must be able to "see" a relay for the connection back to the station to be solid. Due to these limitations, micro-wave links are really only feasible for local or regional reporting.

On a side note, news operations that have invested in (or leased) a heli-copter are subject to the same microwave connection protocols. The signal from a helicopter, however, can be direct (helicopter to the station) since the helicopter is (hopefully) already at a height that will permit a clean "shot" back to the station. However, the signal can be indirect as well (helicopter to a relay to the station).

SATELLITE

Going live on location using a satellite signal is a bit more complex (and expensive) than using a microwave link. However, the process is very similar to an indirect microwave connection – the relay just happens to be a satellite in space. Satellite trucks are more expensive than microwave trucks. Newer satellite units are portable (and can fit in a few equipment cases). However, a satellite system will permit live news reporting from just about anywhere on the planet. Satellite systems are also useful in news markets that are geographically difficult or extend beyond the reach of a microwave system.

A satellite signal will almost always need to be received (tuned and decoded) in Master Control before routing to the Control Room. Once in the Control Room, the audio and video feed from the satellite can be han-dled in the same manner as any other audio and video source.

The Satellite Connection

The common connection from the satellite truck (or portable unit) is indi-rect (truck to the satellite to the station). However, satellite hook-ups are limited (just like microwave is) as a line-of-sight transmission. The truck must be able to "see" the satellite and the satellite must be able to "see" the station.

Once on location, the truck will make the connection to the satellite by "leasing" the time needed for the feed from a third party who owns the satellite. Organizations such as CBS's Newspath and NBC's News

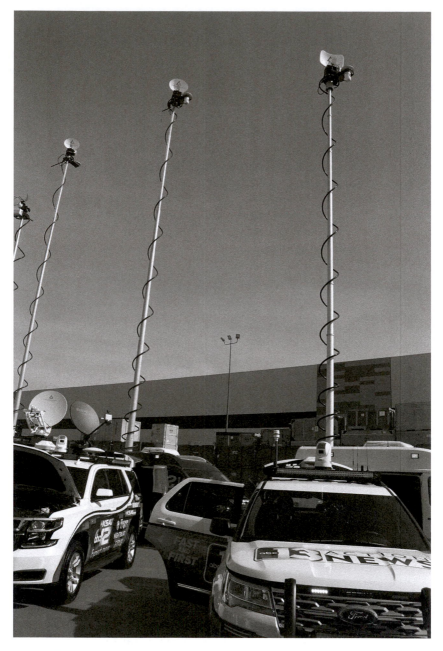

Figure 6.9 Microwave trucks at the NAB Show

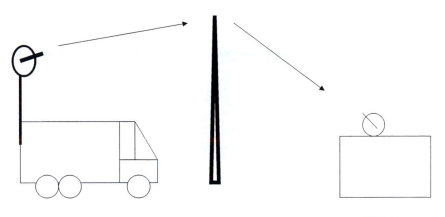

Figure 6.10 Microwave relay schematic

Channel are designed to serve local stations by providing cost-effective satellite time, and a way to share video among the affiliated stations. Stations typically have contracts that govern the cost for time and pay a "flat" per minute fee for it.

INTERNET

The internet has made reporting from remote geographic areas a much simpler technical task. A reporter equipped with a camera and a laptop computer can easily shoot, edit, and voice a story in the field. The segment can be incorporated into the newscast as an "as-live" story.

Once the video file is completed, the file can be sent from any reliable internet connection (coffee shops and hotels seem to be popular transmission locations). As long as the file can be completely transmitted (not blocked by server protocols on file size), a compressed HD news package of up to five minutes in length can be sent through a broadband connection in less than thirty minutes. A more modest connection can be used (cellular) as long as the integrity of the connection can be maintained – although it may take more time. Once a file has started recording at the server, it can begin playback/streaming within seconds, even though the recording may not be complete.

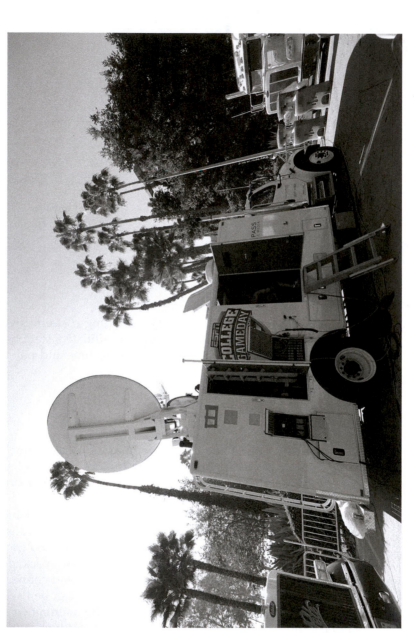

Figure 6.11 Satellite truck, Los Angeles, CA – November 23, 2012 – Los Angeles Memorial Coliseum: on the set of ESPN College Game Day

(Photo by Allen Kee/Courtesy ESPN Images)

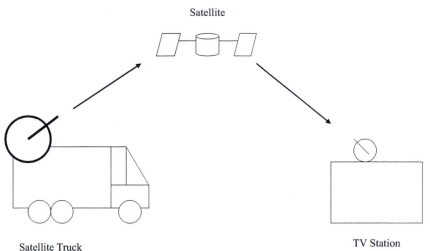

Satellite

Satellite Truck

TV Station

Figure 6.12 Satellite relay schematic

DIRECTING A LIVE REMOTE

The command syntax for directing a Live Remote is really no different from activating any other audio and video source to Program. The major worry with a remote set-up is communication between the technical staff on the ground and the Control Room. A few procedures can be followed to help minimize the communication stress.

Program Feed

First, the folks on location need to be able to see and hear the output of the station – often this is handled on a return feed right through the cellular, microwave, or satellite system itself. A monitor can be hooked up to serve this purpose. Additionally, an IFB bug will need to be connected for the talent to be able to monitor program audio as well as listen to any directions from the producer.

Remote Intercom

Second, the technical folks on location need to be hooked into the intercom system so that they may hear and respond to commands from the Director. Again, this can be handled on a return feed from the station. A cellular phone connection can easily substitute for a true intercom connection.

Cellular

Third, a cell phone connection between the remote unit and the Control Room is a prudent communication safety in case the remote intercom system fails.

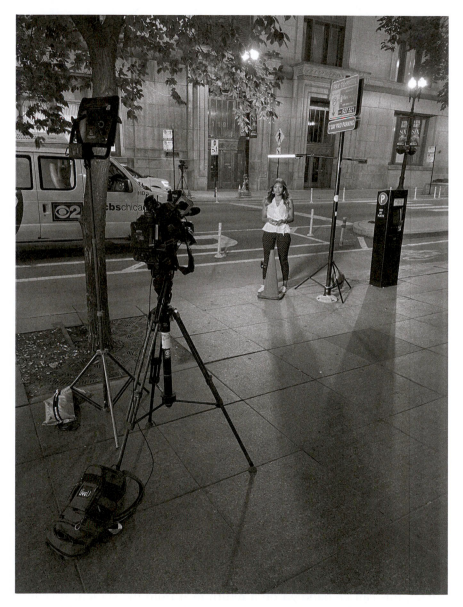

Figure 6.13 Remote set-up; WBBM Channel 2 – CBS Chicago, IL

(Courtesy Jeffry Langan)

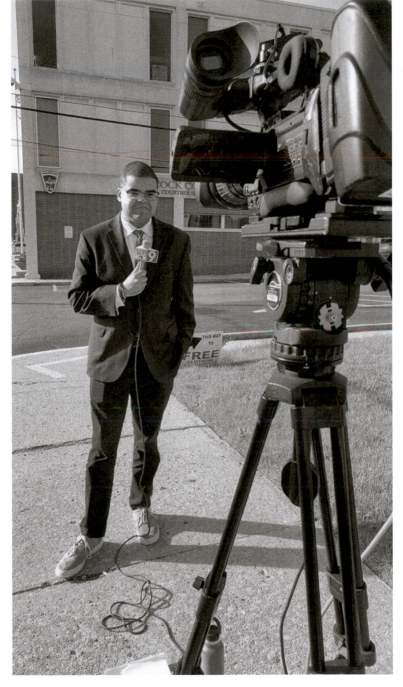

Figure 6.13a Reporter on remote; WTOV Channel 9 – Steubenville, OH
(Courtesy Tyler Madden)

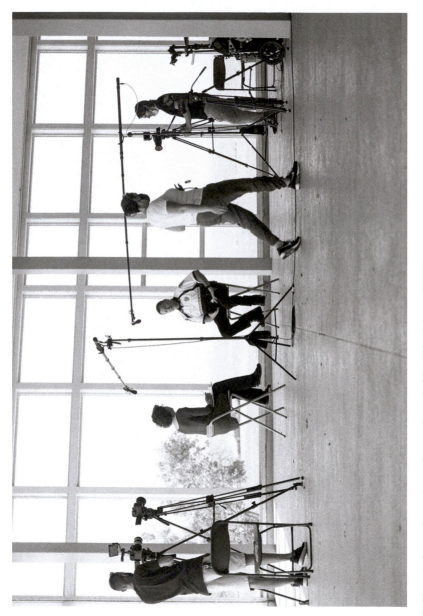

Figure 6.13b Remote interview set-up; Connecticut Public Television – CPTV
(Courtesy David Wurtzel)

ENGINEERING: A SUPER BASIC INTRODUCTION

The Broadcast Engineer is an individual (or a team of individuals) that are vital to the production environment. The list of responsibilities of these individuals is far too lengthy to cover in this section. However, a basic understanding of what they do is important for the entry-level student.

Broadcast Engineers are responsible for signal routing. In the studio environment, audio and video signals are connected from their sources to their destinations using patches, routers, servers, and networks. If remotes are in use, the connections may be wireless (bonded cellular, microwave, satellite) or wired (over IP).

A super basic example of signal routing is a microphone that is hooked into a patch panel in the studio. Let us imagine that a lavaliere microphone is connected using an XLR cable to the patch panel and is "plugged" into an XLR audio jack labelled "Mic #9." The Mic #9 panel wires are connected to the control room to a rack-mounted router. The router can then be programmed to "send" the audio from Mic #9 to an array of locations. Suppose we would like Mic #9 on Fader 2 on the Audio Board. The router would need to be programmed to "send" the audio to that location. The Broadcast Engineer would assist with this routing.

Another common job for the Engineer is to set-up the cameras in the studio. The cameras in use will need to be tuned in such a way that all of them are "seeing" the values of black and white, and reading color in exactly the same manner (at the electromagnetic level). In this way, when we switch from Camera 1 to Camera 2, the color of the Anchor's shirt will not change and the "blacks" will not be too dark and the "whites" will not be overexposed.

The first step in this process is to "balance" the cameras. The cameras need to be "told" what the values of black and white are in a given lighting environment. The old school scale that is used is called "IRE" (Institute of Radio Engineers). The IRE scale is *essentially* zero to one hundred (although readings on the scale *can* go below zero and *can* go above one hundred). In current environments, many engineers prefer to use millivolts (mV) rather than IRE. The scales do correspond (1 IRE is 7.143 mV). Reference Black is 7.5 IRE (53.57 mV); 100 IRE is 714.3 mV – and so forth.

The bottom level (black) needs to be set to a corresponding value of approximately 7.5 IRE (or 53.57mV) on all of the cameras. The IRE can be set slightly lower (4 or 5 IRE) but one does risk "crushing" the black value. What that means is that darker areas in a video image become so dark that they cannot be seen on the screen. And ... one would typically not set the black level at zero (pure black) – although this was the standard in Japan for a time.

In order to work through this the engineer will fire up the lighting grid and aim the cameras at a registration card on the set. Once the cameras are "set" to the black value, the cameras can then be "set" to a white value.

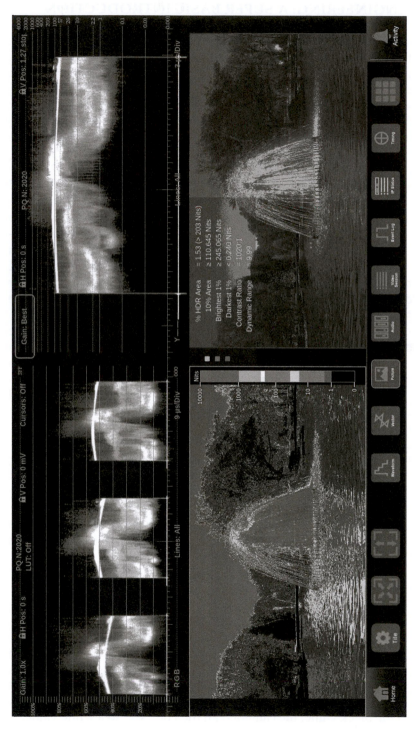

Figure 6.14 (a–c) Engineering test equipment; waveform and exposure monitors, vectorscopes, HDR

(Courtesy Telestream)

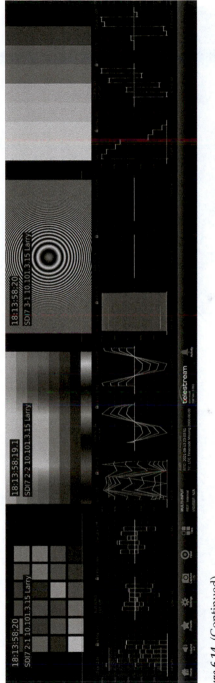

Figure 6.14 (Continued)

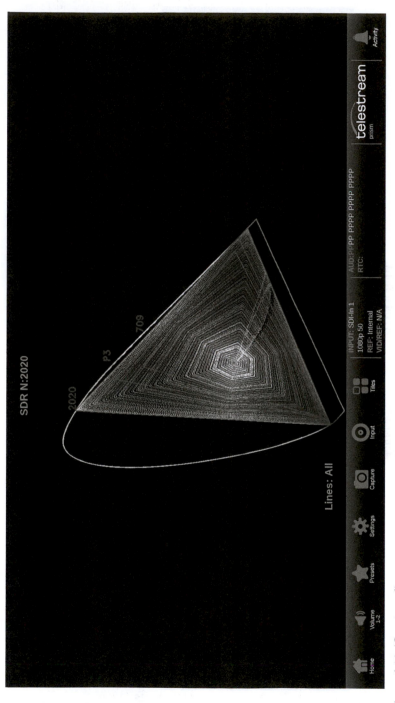

Figure 6.14 (Continued)

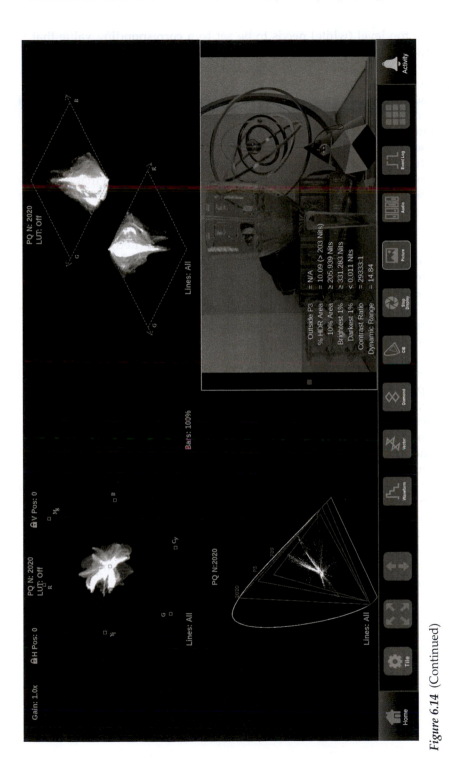

Figure 6.14 (Continued)

The top level (white) needs to be set to a corresponding value that is slightly less than 100 IRE (less than 714.3 mV). The reasoning for this is to allow for some headroom in the video signal for highlights in the image (super whites).

The settings are checked using the WaveForm monitor. Essentially, what the engineer is doing is setting the bottom level (black) and the top level (white) of the video signal from each of the cameras.

The Engineer can then move on to color. The engineer will accomplish this tuning using a vectorscope. Using this tool, the Engineer can see the video signal in relation to color and adjust the cameras so that no colors are "in" the black or "in" the white; and, the engineer can be sure that each camera is seeing color exactly the same way. In a basic set-up, three colors can be adjusted (Red; Green; Blue; this is the RGB standard). In more advanced set-ups, six colors can be adjusted (Red; Magenta; Blue; Cyan; Green; Yellow). Once the cameras are "seeing" in the same way or matched, they are considered to be "balanced."

The nifty thing about these adjustments is that one can use them to "tint" an image for a particular look. For example, the white balance can be tinted toward blue to create a cold look.

Outside of the production process, Broadcast Engineers are responsible for a wide variety of tasks. Engineers design and build studios, control rooms, and master control facilities. Engineers repair all of the electronic equipment (some down to the circuit board level). Engineers set up hardware, software, satellite remotes, microwave remotes, helicopter remotes, servers, local area networks, field production units, full production trucks, and much much more.

And finally, Engineers are responsible for the transmission of the signal out of the television station or network (transmitters, satellite uplinks, cable headends, fiber optic links). Engineers that work on television and radio transmitters and translators are typically licensed by the Federal Communications Commission (FCC). Nowadays, engineers need to be very familiar with all sorts of IT networking including cellular networks and computer networks.

Note: Not *all* engineers "do" *all* of these tasks as many engineering careers are specialized into a few areas.

7

RUNDOWNS, SCRIPTS, VIDEO CLIP INFORMATION

INTRODUCTION

The process of creating any television program begins with the desire to communicate. The complex and unique visual nature of television requires the creative team to visualize the program on paper (or virtual paper) in the pre-production process.

While many tools are available to assist in the visualization process, like storyboarding, the final components that are needed for the production process include the rundown, the script, and a mechanism for conveying video clip information to the production staff.

The rundown is a segment by segment outline of a program. Usually formatted as a chronological list, the rundown will include information about video sourcing, audio sourcing, and timing information regarding each segment.

The script is a written document that contains the stories the anchors are to read. In multi-camera productions, the script is usually formatted in two columns with production information in the left column and the scripting in the right column. The two-column format permits the staff to track not only what the anchor is saying but also what the viewer will be seeing.

Pre-recorded video clips are a common part of most studio-based production. The content the clips may contain is really just about anything you can think of: highlights of a sporting event, footage of a traffic jam, kids picking pumpkins, or video of a tornado. Information for each clip must be made available for the production crew regarding the *location* of the clip (what machine "holds" it and will "play" it), the *name* of the clip (file name or number), the *duration* of the clip (how long it is), the *type* of clip (VO, VO/SOT, or PKG), and any *graphic* requirements (e.g. character generation).

DOI: 10.4324/9780429244100-7

The following section describes the three primary components needed for the production process: rundowns, scripts, and video clip information.

However, prior to proceeding with the material in this chapter, it is important to note that a specific Newsroom Computer System – the unique combination of software/hardware found in a given installation – will manage each component in a slightly different manner. Yet, to surf the internet with Safari is not so different than surfing with Chrome, Firefox, or any other "browser." Essentially, the student will need to learn the specific workflows of any given NRCS in a hands-on environment.

THE RUNDOWN

A news **rundown** (running order) is a rough outline or chart indicating the technical elements required for a specific program. Everyone on the production crew should receive a copy of the rundown prior to the show. Knowing how to decipher a rundown, therefore, is important to all members of the crew.

In the most basic form, a rundown must convey the following information: segment number or identifier (RUN), the primary video source for the segment (VID), video clip location if a roll-in is associated with the segment (L), the primary audio source for the segment (AUD), the segment or story slug (SLUG), the amount of time the segment is expected to run (SEG), and a total running time column for the entire program (TRT).

It is important to note that a wide variety of rundown forms are in use in the television news industry. Many rundowns are more complex than the one described here or are unique to a given program.

SEGMENT NUMBER (RUN)

The first column in the rundown (RUN) conveys the **segment number** or segment identifier. In the example here, each segment is identified by a 100, 200, 300, or 400 series number.

Each series of numbers is called a **block** (one might say, "the three-hundred block is weather"). Each block is separated by a commercial break. Normally, there are four blocks to the half hour (although this varies) and within a block, one could have up to 99 events (101 to 199). The numbering logic within a block is rarely in perfect sequence (101, 102, 103) to allow for the addition of a new segment (breaking news for example) without requiring the entire rundown and the associated media assets to be re-numbered.

It is very common in the industry to use an alternate form of run number that uses the alphabet as block identifiers (A block, B block, C block) and

iNEWS - [[KRCG]ARCHIVE.2015.JAN.06.P-CONGRESS RETURNS]

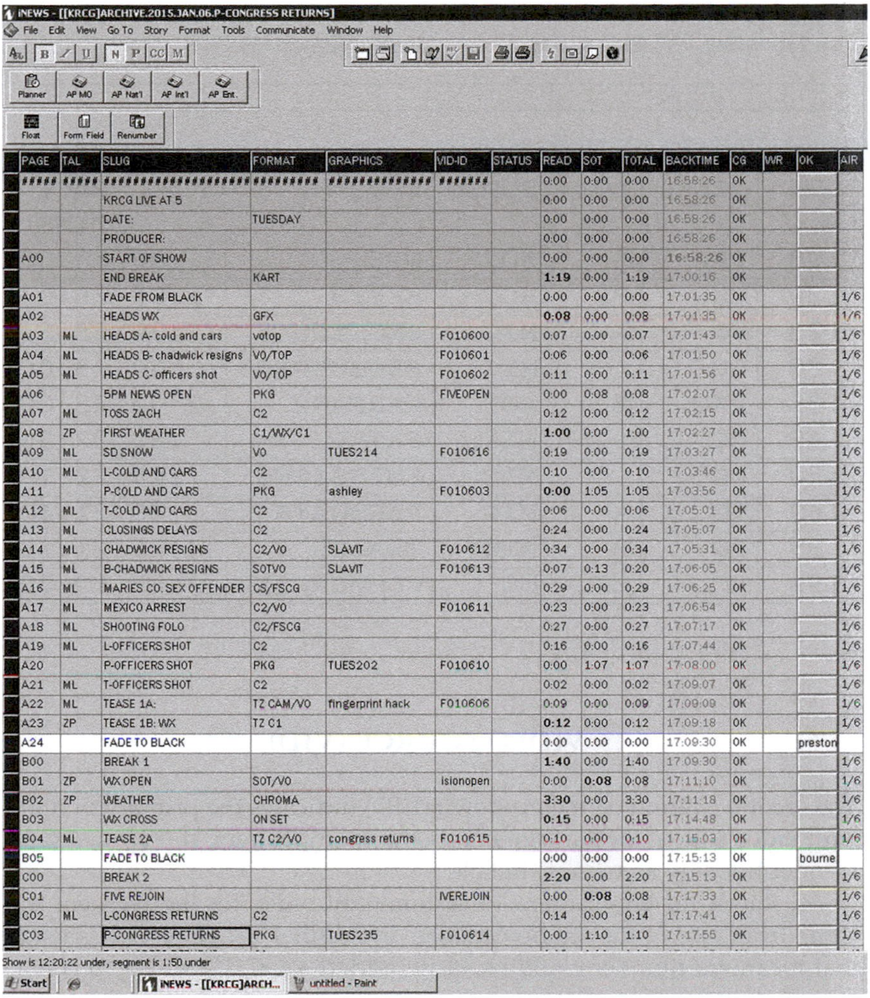

File Edit View Go To Story Format Tools Communicate Window Help

PAGE	TAL	SLUG	FORMAT	GRAPHICS	VID-ID	STATUS	READ	SOT	TOTAL	BACKTIME	CG	WR	OK	AIR
#####	#####	############################ ########	###############	########			0:00	0:00	0:00	16:58:26	OK			
		KRCG LIVE AT 5					0:00	0:00	0:00	16:58:26	OK			
		DATE:	TUESDAY				0:00	0:00	0:00	16:58:26	OK			
		PRODUCER:					0:00	0:00	0:00	16:58:26	OK			
A00		START OF SHOW					0:00	0:00	0:00	16:58:26	OK			
		END BREAK	KART				1:19	0:00	1:19	17:00:16	OK			
A01		FADE FROM BLACK					0:00	0:00	0:00	17:01:35	OK			1/6
A02		HEADS WX	GFX				0:08	0:00	0:08	17:01:35	OK			1/6
A03	ML	HEADS A- cold and cars	votop		F010600		0:07	0:00	0:07	17:01:43	OK			1/6
A04	ML	HEADS B- chadwick resigns	V0/TOP		F010601		0:06	0:00	0:06	17:01:50	OK			1/6
A05	ML	HEADS C- officers shot	V0/TOP		F010602		0:11	0:00	0:11	17:01:56	OK			1/6
A06		5PM NEWS OPEN	PKG		FIVEOPEN		0:00	0:08	0:08	17:02:07	OK			1/6
A07	ML	TOSS ZACH	C2				0:12	0:00	0:12	17:02:15	OK			1/6
A08	ZP	FIRST WEATHER	C1/WX/C1				1:00	0:00	1:00	17:02:27	OK			1/6
A09	ML	SD SNOW	VO	TUES214	F010616		0:19	0:00	0:19	17:03:27	OK			1/6
A10	ML	L-COLD AND CARS	C2				0:10	0:00	0:10	17:03:46	OK			1/6
A11		P-COLD AND CARS	PKG	ashley	F010603		0:00	1:05	1:05	17:03:56	OK			1/6
A12	ML	T-COLD AND CARS	C2				0:06	0:00	0:06	17:05:01	OK			1/6
A13	ML	CLOSINGS DELAYS	C2				0:24	0:00	0:24	17:05:07	OK			1/6
A14	ML	CHADWICK RESIGNS	C2/VO	SLAVIT	F010612		0:34	0:00	0:34	17:05:31	OK			1/6
A15	ML	B-CHADWICK RESIGNS	SOTVO	SLAVIT	F010613		0:07	0:13	0:20	17:06:05	OK			1/6
A16	ML	MARIES CO. SEX OFFENDER	CS/FSCG				0:29	0:00	0:29	17:06:25	OK			1/6
A17	ML	MEXICO ARREST	C2/VO		F010611		0:23	0:00	0:23	17:06:54	OK			1/6
A18	ML	SHOOTING FOLO	C2/FSCG				0:27	0:00	0:27	17:07:17	OK			1/6
A19	ML	L-OFFICERS SHOT	C2				0:16	0:00	0:16	17:07:44	OK			1/6
A20		P-OFFICERS SHOT	PKG	TUES202	F010610		0:00	1:07	1:07	17:08:00	OK			1/6
A21	ML	T-OFFICERS SHOT	C2				0:02	0:00	0:02	17:09:07	OK			1/6
A22	ML	TEASE 1A:	TZ CAM/VO	fingerprint hack	F010606		0:09	0:00	0:09	17:09:09	OK			1/6
A23	ZP	TEASE 1B: WX	TZ C1				0:12	0:00	0:12	17:09:18	OK			1/6
A24		FADE TO BLACK					0:00	0:00	0:00	17:09:30	OK	preston		
B00		BREAK 1					1:40	0:00	1:40	17:09:30	OK			1/6
B01	ZP	WX OPEN	SOT/VO		isionopen		0:00	0:08	0:08	17:11:10	OK			1/6
B02	ZP	WEATHER	CHROMA				3:30	0:00	3:30	17:11:18	OK			1/6
B03		WX CROSS	ON SET				0:15	0:00	0:15	17:14:48	OK			1/6
B04	ML	TEASE 2A	TZ C2/VO	congress returns	F010615		0:10	0:00	0:10	17:15:03	OK			1/6
B05		FADE TO BLACK					0:00	0:00	0:00	17:15:13	OK	bourne		
C00		BREAK 2					2:20	0:00	2:20	17:15:13	OK			1/6
C01		FIVE REJOIN			IVEREJOIN		0:00	0:08	0:08	17:17:33	OK			1/6
C02	ML	L-CONGRESS RETURNS	C2				0:14	0:00	0:14	17:17:41	OK			1/6
C03		P-CONGRESS RETURNS	PKG	TUES235	F010614		0:00	1:10	1:10	17:17:55	OK			1/6

Show is 12:20:22 under, segment is 1:50 under

Start   iNEWS - [[KRCG]ARCH...   untitled - Paint

Figure 7.1 Avid iNews screen grab of rundown

(Courtesy Robby Messer, KRCG)

numbers for specific segments (A-1, A-2, A-3). On many news programs, certain events happen every time the show airs. For example, the show teaser (indicated as run number 98) is an event that occurs every time the show airs. As such, it is a "fixed" item on the rundown. Run number 99, the show open (usually a pre-produced package of video, graphics, and music) is another example of an event that is fixed ("… and now, live from Baltimore, Eyewitness News!").

```
RUNDOWN
SHOW: NEWS   TIME: FINAL        DATE: MARCH 21
```

						28:30
RUN #	VIDEO	LOC	AUDIO	SLUG	TIME	BACK TIME
100	PKG	A	SOT	OPEN	:30	28:00
120	PKG	B	SOT	KEYES	2:00	26:00
125	VO	A	MIC	SMOKING	:30	25:30
130	OC		MIC	SENBUDGET	:30	25:00
135	PKG	B	SOT	WARFARE	2:00	23:00
145	OC		MIC	FATAL	:30	22:30
150	OC		MIC	EMISSIONS	:20	22:10
160	VO	A	MIC	PARKWAYS	:30	21:40
198	VO	B	MIC	TEASER	:15	21:25
199	MC	MC	MC	COMMERCIAL	2:25	19:00

Figure 7.2 A basic rundown

VIDEO SOURCE (VID)

The second column on the rundown (VID) indicates the primary or domi-nant video source for the segment. In the example here, six types of video are identified by acronyms/initials.

OC stands for **On-Camera** – the dominant video for the segment is to come from one of the studio cameras. In another usage of OC, consider that a camera number could be easily added – OC 1, OC 2 – to convey more detailed information.

OC story segments are often called "readers" since the anchor is basi-cally reading "to" the camera."

One variation on the reader is the addition of keyed graphics that com-plement the story. For example, a story about a fire might include a lower third CG that indicates to the viewer when/where the fire event hap-pened. Another common variation is add the "box" – aka a "box shot" – where an image (or other graphic) is keyed over the camera shot to one side of the frame.

Types of Pre-Recorded Video Clips (VO, VO-SOT, PKG)

VO or **Voice-Over** indicates that a clip of pre-recorded video is to be the primary video source for the segment. The clip could be played-back from a wide variety of specific devices (playback machines) depending on the configuration of the control room one is working in (our example assumes the use of individual DDRs for playback).

VO, then, is a particular form of news story involving a video clip. In Voice-Over, the video in use for the segment will be spoken-over ("voiced") by the anchor live in the studio – *while the video clip is playing*. Usually a VO begins OC with the anchor reading an introduction to the story segment and is followed by a quick "roll" and cut to video for the VO portion – the anchor keeps reading – and then (sometimes) a cut back to camera for a concluding remark – sometimes called a **tag**. Additional audio may be available to complement the video clip – natural sound or NAT sound (atmosphere).

Variations on a VO are common. The complementary video that is rolled in the VO portion may be event specific or non-event specific. If the video clip is material that was actually acquired at a specific event related to the story, it is event specific.

For example, perhaps the Sports Anchor is doing a VO about a soccer game between Stanford and UCONN. The story would typically begin with the anchor on camera telling the viewers about the game. As the anchor continues to read, video *of that game* would be rolled and cut into program. The viewer, then, would be seeing the video of the game but *still hearing* the sports anchor. Often, the anchor will be voicing the "high-lights" – the "plays" of the game – and the script will be "play by play." The video may or may not have NAT sound.

If the video clip in a VO is not material that was actually acquired at a specific event it is called non-event specific footage. Non-event specific footage is video that is complementary but is not from – or of – the actual event. When a VO type of video clip uses non-event specific footage, it is called "file" footage and really must be identified as such (a simple CG over the video that says FILE is adequate). Often, an event happens in a location where getting video of the actual event is impossible or simply not feasible. In that case, using file footage makes sense.

What is file footage? File footage is "old" or "generic" video of all sorts of things (a traffic jam, people walking down the sidewalks of New York City, footage of waves crashing onto a beach, footage of a thunderstorm with lightning, drone video of the downtown area of a city, etc.).

For example, imagine that a helicopter crashes into the Grand Canyon. If no footage is available, basic file footage of the Grand Canyon could be used to complement the story. In this way, one can convert an OC "reader" fairly easily into a VO. Again, the video portion may or may not have NAT sound.

VO/SOT (Voice-Over followed by **Sound-on-Tape**) also indicates that a clip of pre-recorded video will be the primary video source for the segment. The VO/SOT is a close cousin to the VO, popular in sports news, and is also a type of pre-recorded video clip.

Usually a VO/SOT begins OC with the anchor reading an introduction followed by a quick "roll" and cut to video for the VO portion – the anchor keeps reading – and then, at a pre-timed point on the clip, an edit occurs to a sound-bite (SOT). The anchor stops reading, the audio will switch from the anchor's mic to the clip audio – and the SOT portion (note on SOT – old school – actually is referencing Sound-on-Tape) plays itself out. At the conclusion of the SOT portion of the VO/SOT, a cut back to camera for a concluding remark or "tag" from the anchor is common. Again, during the VO portion of the clip, additional audio may be available to complement the video – natural sound or NAT sound (atmosphere).

OC	ON-CAMERA
VO	VOICE-OVER
VO/SOT	VOICE-OVER FOLLOWED BY SOUND-ON-TAPE
SOT/VO	SOUND-ON-TAPE FOLLOWED BY VOICE-OVER
PKG	PACKAGE
FX or FS	GRAPHICS OR EFFECTS SEQUENCE
ESS	ELECTRONIC STILL-STORE
CG	CHARACTER GENERATOR
LIVE	MICROWAVE OR SATELLITE REMOTE
MX	MICROWAVE
SAT	SATELLITE
DVE	DIGITAL VIDEO EFFECTS
MC	MASTER CONTROL
CAM	CAMERA
CAM 1	CAMERA ONE
KEY	KEY SHOT
REM	REMOTE

Figure 7.3 Chart of video related initials

The VO portion of the clip is almost always event-specific footage. However, the VO portion *could* use non-event specific footage – but it would be unusual.

It is important to point out that VO/SOTs *have many forms* – the VO/SOT/VO; the SOT/VO; the SOT/VO/SOT; and so on. The concept to remember at this point is that the VO/SOT is a form of news story involving a video clip as the primary video source.

Don't forget!

The VO/SOT is easily *reversed* to the SOT/VO ...
The VO/SOT is easily *expanded* to the VO/SOT/VO
The SOT/VO is easily expanded to the SOT/VO/SOT
And, look out for the MOS which is really a SOT/SOT/SOT/SOT/SOT and/or the VO/SOT/SOT or SOT/SOT/VO ...

VIDEO SOURCE (VID) II

PKG or Package indicates that a clip of pre-recorded video is to be the primary video source for the segment. In this form, the video and audio are all "packaged" or produced together on the clip.

Typically, an anchor opens a PKG with a live introduction from the studio (OC) followed by a quick "roll" and cut to video for the PKG. While the video clip is playing, the anchor is standing by – usually watching the package on a monitor and listening to the audio track on the IFB. At the conclusion of the clip, the anchor usually gives a concluding remark or tag (OC) before moving on to the next story.

A common variation on the PKG protocol is to have the anchor introduce a reporter in the field "live," and to permit the field reporter to introduce and tag the package from a remote location (bonded cellular, microwave, or satellite).

Packages tend to be constructed in two ways. A symmetrical package is where the internal elements follow a pattern. An asymmetrical package is where the internal elements generally do not follow a pattern.

For the beginning student, constructing packages *using a pattern* is a great "recipe" to follow.

Symmetrical Package:

Opening Stand-Up
Voice-Over
SOT (soundbite)
Middle Stand-Up
Voice-Over

SOT (soundbite)
Closing Stand-Up.

Once a student is more familiar with the basic recipe, many more audio and video ingredients can be included (and these ingredients are only limited by your imagination!).

Asymmetrical Package:

Nat-Pop
Voice-Over
SOT (soundbite) w/cutaway
SOT (soundbite)
Voice-Over
Map Graphic with SOT (soundbite)
Voice-Over
Closing Stand-Up.

One super useful exercise for all students of television news is to not only watch the news but to "diagram" the news. One exercise is to re-create the rundown. Another is to diagram packages. Just as one can diagram a sentence by identifying the subject, the direct object, the predicate verb, and so-forth, one can diagram a package (shot by shot, element by element) in order to better understand how packages are constructed.

Other VID

Several other acronyms or initials are commonly deployed in the VID column. CG stands for Character Generator – the primary video source of computer-generated text of some kind. ESS stands for Electronic Still-Store – a picture or graphics file of some kind, also coming from a computer or from the switcher. **FX** (or **FS**) is a generic indicator for Effects or Graphics. Again, the most likely video source would be a Control Room computer for FX or FS. KEY commonly stands for an over-the-shoulder box graphic. REM, SAT, LIVE, or Live-Inject indicates a live-shot.

DVE stands for Digital Video Effects. In DVE, a video source (or two, or three) is assigned to a special effects box that manipulates the source in some fashion. A good example of this is when two cameras are assigned to the DVE to create a split-screen effect so that reporters in different locations may seem to interact with one another on-screen.

MC stands for Master Control (aka Transmission Control). When indicated as a primary video source on a run down, it means that the video for the segment will be handled remotely from the Control Room. Commercials, for example, are usually "rolled" from the Master Control area in the station.

Whatever the acronym or initials, remember that the VID column is all about the video source. Depending on the show, the station, or the network, a wide variety of indicators may appear in this column.

LOCATION (L)

The **L** column conveys **Location**. Historically, the column tells the reader the specific name of the machine that holds the video clip. When more than one playback device is to be utilized, the location column must be used to identify which specific playback device "holds" the video clip. DDRs are usually lettered (DDRA, DDRB) or numbered (DDR1023, DDR4092) depending on the protocol in use at the station. Note: many Directors prefer letters to numbers as identifiers for the playback machines to avoid confusion with the cameras.

The locations are a *technical* part of the execution of the program. Typically the locations are alternated ABAB, or ABCABC, depending on how many playback devices or channels of playback (server) are available. Location alternation helps both the TD and the Audio Operator to know where the next clip will be played (or sourced) from.

Today, it is not uncommon for one machine (a clip server of some kind) to hold all of the pre-recorded clips. In this instance, the clips are always coming from the same machine and the location column is typically repurposed to identify the file name of the clip and/or the specific server video channel.

So, if a segment on a rundown is to utilize a pre-recorded video clip (this would include the VO, VO/SOT, or PKG), a Location (or file name) would be expected. Logically, if a segment utilizes no video clip – an OC for instance – no Location information should appear on the rundown.

The L column is taking on a new role as the Control Room world expands to include video clips sourced from multiple playback devices. It is important to remember that if a pre-recorded video clip is involved with a segment, it has to come from a specific machine that can be clearly identified and easily called upon.

AUDIO (AUD)

The AUD column indicates the primary or dominant audio source that is in play for the segment. Like the VID column, acronyms and initials are used to identify specific technical devices or protocols as audio sources.

MIC stands for Microphone (easily expanded to convey more information – MIC5, MIC1). SOT stands for Sound-On-Tape. The primary audio source in a SOT is the specific device shown in the Location column for the segment. For example, if a PKG is in DDRA the audio for the clip is also DDRA.

As shown in the example rundown, many audio sources are automatically associated with a given video source. For example, if the dominant video is OC, logically, the primary audio is going to be MIC. If the dominant video is PKG, the primary audio is going to be SOT.

SLUG (SLUG)

The **SLUG** (Item) column is merely indicating another identifier for the segment. A slug is a short name given to the segment by the producing staff earlier in the news day and usually prior to the final creation of the rundown. Slugs can also be merely informative – see 199, "Commercial Break #1."

A good indicator of whether a person is on the production team or on the producing staff is how that person refers to a segment. Production folks will say, "we are in 105 and 110 is next." A producer might say, "we are in Fire and Traffic is next." Only major technical segments (usually a given news story) get a line on the rundown. Minor or fleeting technical tasks within a story (changing from camera to a playback device for example) do not typically get a separate line. If such were the case, the rundown for a typical news program would be very long indeed.

TIMING (SEG AND TRT)

The final two columns indicate timing information. The first of these, SEG, is indicating the producer's estimate as to how long the entire segment will take. SEG time is inclusive of anchor introductions, video clips, and tags (if any). So, if a video clip associated with a segment is 15 seconds long, one must add the introduction time and tag time to the **clip time** to figure out SEG time.

For example, if the introduction will take 5 seconds, the video clip 15 seconds, and the tag 10 seconds – the SEG time would be :30.

The final column, **TRT**, stands for **Total Running Time** for the program. TRT will be indicated in one of two forms, either additive or subtractive. Additive TRT, as is used here, begins at zero and merely adds SEG time at each line. Subtractive TRT begins with the expected total length of the program and subtracts each SEG in sequence (for example 30:00 minus :10 is 29:50 minus 1:30 is 28:20 and so on).

The form of TRT really depends on the protocols in play at your facility. TRT is vital to the AD and Producer. At the end of every segment, using TRT and a Master Clock, one can figure if the show is running long (too much material and/or too slow) or short (not enough material and/or too fast).

Newsroom software suites, like Octopus, often build-in a timing function that will handle Total Running Time.

READING IS FUNDAMENTAL

The ability to decipher a rundown is vital to all members of the production crew. While the basic form conveyed here should more than suffice to begin your rundown literacy, you should be encouraged to seek out and learn about other forms that are in use or common to a particular genre of program. No one form of rundown is the "correct" one. The important point to remember is that a rundown needs to communicate, clearly, the technical requirements of the program to the crew.

SCRIPTING

Scripting is a producing function – writing – that has a good deal of impact on how a Director actually "calls" or cues a program. The standard format for news is a two-column script. The first column indicates production information. The right hand column is where the actual script (what the anchor's will say) is located. The organization protocol for the script will follow the protocol of the rundown.

As a news show is created, not only is the script written, but the show is visualized by the producing staff – not only what the viewer will hear but what the viewer will see is determined. The script, therefore, needs to reflect both.

Integrated newsroom software, like ENPS or Octopus, is a useful tool in creating the rundown and the script at the same time. Multiple users (writers, reporters, producers) can access all of the scripts from any newsroom computer to make changes in the running order, edits, or to add information. As will be shown in Chapter 8, the script will become the primary tool the Director will use to "call" or "cue" the program.

VIDEO CLIP INFORMATION

On average, a separate video clip will be rolled into a news program every minute. Technical information concerning each clip needs to be conveyed to the production crew in an efficient and logical manner. However, of all of the "ways of doing things" in the industry, none is more varied than the vehicle for conveying video clip information to the staff.

No matter what technique is utilized, the following information regarding each clip needs to be communicated. Beyond the basics – what show, what day, what time – one of the first items to consider is to what story or production segment (run number) is the clip associated with? What is the precise length of the clip? What kind of audio is on the clip? Do graphics need to be created to be layered over the clip? If so, what

```
120 – Figure Skating


CAM 3
                                  Olympic Gold Medalist
                                  Alexei Yaguden (AH LEX AY
                                  YAH GOO DEN) is coming to
                                  perform this weekend at
                                  Eastern Connecticut State
                                  University.
TAKE VO
                                  Yaguden, the 2002 Olympic
:32                               Gold Medalist is on tour in
                                  North America for the next
                                  year in the attempt to
                                  raise money for the
                                  Struggling Russian
                                  Gymnastics program.
                                  Yaguden, who is married to
                                  the Russian Figure Skating
                                  Champion Bakarov (BAHK R
                                  OFF), is also trying to
                                  raise money for the other
                                  Russian teams who are also
                                  facing shortfalls. The
                                  Russian government, once
                                  well known for its support
                                  of Olympic athletes, has,
                                  in recent years, cut off
                                  all funding to the teams.
                                  Numerous athletes from the
                                  former Soviet Union have
                                  immigrated to other
                                  countries in search of
                                  financial support for
                                  training.  Most have landed
                                  in the U.S. although the
                                  athletes continue to
                                  compete for Russia.

                                  ###
```

Figure 7.4 A basic two-column script

are they and precisely when in the duration of the clip are they to be layered (or keyed) over? What kind of story form is the clip (VO, VO/SOT,
PKG)? If the clip is on a physical piece of media, what piece of media is
the clip located on; and, where on that physical piece of media is the clip
located? If the clip is on a server, on which server channel is it and what
is the name of the file?

FONT SHEET

RUN #_____   DATE:_____

SLUG:_____   TAPE #:_____

PRODUCER:_____   CUT#:_____

NATSOUND (circle): CH1   CH2   TRT with PAD:_____

****

Story Type: VO   VO/SOT   SOT/VO   VO/SOT/VO   SOT/VO/SOT   PKG
 (circle)

                 SEG. TIME

VO   _____

PKG/SOT   _____   OUTCUE:_____

VO   _____

SOT   _____   OUTCUE:_____

****

TIME   FONT

_____   _____

_____   _____

_____   _____

_____   _____

_____   _____

_____   _____

Figure 7.5 A basic font or clip sheet

FONT SHEET OR CLIP SHEET

One older technique to convey clip information is to consolidate it onto one form – a **font sheet** (clip sheet) – or some similar document. The older font sheet technique is, perhaps, *the best way to learn the basics* about clip information. The document may be in hard copy form, embedded in the rundown, embedded in the script, accessible on a network, or "all of the above."

If you examine the example provided, you will notice that the top one-third of the form concerns show, tape, and clip information – including total running time (TRT). The middle-third of the form is primarily designed to convey information concerning the type of clip and the timing of the clip elements. Finally, the bottom-third is where graphics information (graphics associated with a video clip) can be timed and written out.

The Top

The top one-third of the font sheet begins with a space for the run number – the segment identifier that the video clip belongs to. The date, slug, and producer are self-explanatory.

The **drive number** information refers to an identifying number that has been assigned to a physical DDR drive in the television station. Often, this number may contain four or more digits (#1057 or #10578) and reflects the logistics (the protocol) of that station. For example, a four-digit numbering system permits a containment of 9,999 physical pieces of media – a five-digit numbering system allows for management of 99,999 physical pieces of media, and so on.

The **cut number** refers to a specific clip on the identified media. Since most video clips for television news rarely exceed three minutes, many clips are loaded (or edited) onto any specific media drive (sometimes these drives are called edit masters). For example, a drive number of 1010 and a clip number of 7 indicates that the desired clip is on drive 1010 and the file name is "7" – or the desired video is the seventh clip (or file) loaded on the drive.

The next line provides space to indicate the presence of **natural sound** (atmosphere) if any. If the clip has NAT (natural sound) isolated onto a specific audio channel, it will be indicated here.

TRT with PAD provides space for the total running time of the clip, including PAD. **PAD** is extra material on the end of the video clip that is present but is not really intended for use.

For example, suppose a story is to air concerning holiday traffic. A producer might use some stock footage of a traffic jam to illustrate the story. If the traffic jam clip is 1 minute and the script for the story will only take the anchor 20 seconds to read, you have a situation where the clip has 40 seconds of PAD – extra material that is not really needed, but present.

Directors and Assistant Directors can use that extra time to smooth out or ease the transition from the clip back to the studio.

FONT SHEET OR CLIP SHEET II

The Middle

The middle portion of the font sheet is redundant, to some extent, with portions of the rundown. Although it is provided for in this example font sheet, the rundown also would indicate the story type in the VID column.

Seg time refers to segment time within a clip. If the clip is a VO (and only a VO), one would expect a time to be indicated to the right of the VO indicator. If the clip is a PKG (and only a PKG), one would expect a time to be indicated to the right of the PKG indicator (and so on).

However, suppose a clip is a VO/SOT. The specific length of the VO portion and the exact time of the SOT needs to be conveyed. Both indicators, in this instance, would contain time information. A common protocol, and variation on this is to convey time information in the body of the script.

The space to indicate an **outcue** applies primarily to packages and or VO/SOTs or variations that end in SOT. The outcue is the last thing heard (or seen) at the end of the video clip. Knowing the outcue permits the Director (and the rest of the crew) to transition out of a video clip as tightly as possible. It is not uncommon to the see the word "standard" or (STD) written-in as an outcue (or SIG/SIG Out – "sign off" or "signature"). A standard outcue is merely the reporter's name and station identification (in either order). "For the PBS News Hour, I'm Stephen Timothy," or "I'm Matthew Evans, MSNBC …"

FONT SHEET OR CLIP SHEET III

The Bottom

If the clip requires character generation to be keyed over live (and many news clips do), the content of that CG and the expected time it is needed can be conveyed similar to what is shown on the bottom of the example font sheet.

The time indicator would be based from the absolute beginning of the clip (a :07 means 7 seconds into the clip – a 1:09 means one minute and 9 seconds into the clip, etc.). The expected content would be jotted into the space to the right of the time indicator so that the content can be screened prior to the activation of the key layer. A duration for the graphic should be noted so as to prevent the wrong graphic from overlapping the next shot.

With the widespread use of non-linear editing systems, it is not uncommon to find video clips with all of the character generation pre-edited. If this protocol is in place at a given news operation, the job (and stress level) of the Director, the AD, the Graphics operator, and the TD can be greatly reduced.

The Variations

Another technique to convey clip information is to locate it more readily and target it to the production staff that require it. For example, the duration of a clip, most readily required by the Director and Assistant Director, might be located in the left-hand column of the script. Graphic requirements could be handled with a separate form that originates with the producing staff, the editing staff, or both. An expanded rundown could also handle some necessary information regarding any given clip. The concept to remember is that key information regarding the video clip must be conveyed in some manner to the production staff that require it.

8

ASSISTANT DIRECTING AND DIRECTING

ASSISTANT DIRECTING

The process of managing the technical requirements of a live television newscast falls primarily to the Director. A large part of the job of Directing is "knowing what to say and when to say it." Therefore, the Assistant Director's contribution to the process really is significant in terms of figuring out "when to say it." Assistant Directors are responsible for timing.

Show Time

The Assistant Director is responsible for timing the show – forwards and backwards. The AD can announce, at any given moment, how much time has elapsed into the show, and, how much time remains. For example, the AD might announce, "we are 10 minutes 10 seconds into the show, and we have 19 minutes 50 seconds remaining."

In order to control and calculate **show time**, the AD will refer to two clocks (usually located prominently in the control room) – a clock that shows real time (the time of day) that is typically calibrated via satellite or by using the internet. Real time is exact. The network and the local station are often coordinated to the tenth of a second.

The other clock is a large format counter that will be activated at the very beginning of the newscast. The counter will either count up from zero or be pre-set with a duration (28:30 is a common example) and begin to count down when activated. Thus, everyone that can see either clock can coordinate with the AD in terms of the timing of the entire program.

If the show is running short (not enough material), segments can be added or extended (ever wonder why the weather segment and sportscast vary so much in length?). If the show is running long (too much material or a lot of breaking news is added), segments can be deleted ("killed") or

DOI: 10.4324/9780429244100-8

shortened (like the 45 second weather forecast). The show must end precisely so that the station can remain aligned with feeds from the network. (The NBC Nightly News is not going to "wait" for a station in Riverton, Wyoming to "finish" the local newscast).

TIMING VIDEO CLIPS

The other timing task the AD will typically contend with concerns the video clips. Each clip needs to be timed. The Director (and everyone else) needs to know exactly when a clip is ending so that a transition to the next audio and video source may be made smoothly.

The timing information on the clip can be communicated to the AD in any number of ways (on the script, on a clip sheet, in a column on the rundown, or embedded in the NCS). As soon as a clip begins, the AD will normally activate a stopwatch.

By subtracting the stopwatch indication from the clip time, the AD knows "how much time is left" in the video clip. Believe it or not, this "backtiming" task is fairly difficult. Doing math on the fly in this manner is rarely simple. For example, take a normal digital stopwatch and start it from zero. Now, imagine you are timing a clip of 1:23 (one minute, twenty-three seconds in length). Glance at the watch, do the math, and convey the result (out loud). By the time most folks say it, the information is incorrect.

Programmable counters can be used if the time gap between clips is great enough to permit the AD to program in the next clip length and activate a countdown. In many news environments, this is not the case. To get around this problem, many ADs continue to utilize analog stopwatches (like the 60 minutes watch) to work out the timing of video clips. To "do the math" with an analog watch is much easier as the calculation is partially visual (see Figure 8.1).

We Don't Need an AD

It is important to point out that in small and some medium market television news operations, show timing functions fall to a newscast producer. In this scenario, clip timing will more than likely be handled "automatically" by the NCS software or "manually" by the Director. Simply put, the AD job does not exist as a separate crew position at many small and medium market stations.

VO/SOT

Not only is the AD concerned with the length of each clip, the AD must also account for clips that may be broken into VO portions that are edited

Backtiming

The task of backtiming and forward timing a television program is the responsibility of an Assistant Director (or Production Assistant). In the absence of an AD, it is common for the newscast Producer to handle show timing.

Timing the program is usually handled with a simple digital clock. Either one starts the clock from zero and allows it to count up or one sets the expected duration of the show on the clock and allows it to count down.

In either case, the AD should be able to tell how much time has elapsed and how much time is left at-a-glance.

Pre-recorded video clips need to be timed as well. The duration of the clip is the first concern.

In the VO/SOT type of clip, a second concern is the precise moment the SOT portion will commence. Audio will need to track the audio from the tape at this exact moment; and, the anchor will need to be finished speaking.

Finally, the third matter of timing a clip concerns the windows of time when CG can be keyed over the tape (for name, location, or other information).

To handle these three timing tasks, it is common for Assistant Directors to use an analog stopwatch (like the 60 Minutes watch) that features a sweeping second hand. The first task is handled by a process of visual math. The latter two concerns can be handled by merely reading the watch as it counts up from zero.

Visual math is a procedure by which, at-a-glance, the AD can subtract the amount of time elapsed in a tape clip – from the known total running time of the tape clip – with the result of the time remaining in the clip.

To begin the process, the AD makes a mental note of the total running time of the clip. If the clip is 1:23, the AD visually imprints a line across the watch face that crosses through the 25-second mark (see Figure 8.1).

Next the AD visually imprints a perpendicular line to the first (see Figure 8.2) with the result of a cross.

Each quarter of the watch face represents 15 seconds.

When the watch is started from zero, the second hand will begin sweeping toward the first line. When it arrives, 1:15 seconds is left in the tape clip.

When the second hand reaches the second line, 1 minute is left in the tape clip.

When the second hand reaches the third line, 45 seconds is left in the tape clip (and so on).

Figure 8.1a Backtiming Instructions

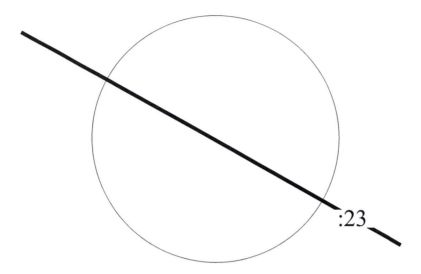

Figure 8.1b The AD will imagine this line across the watch face first

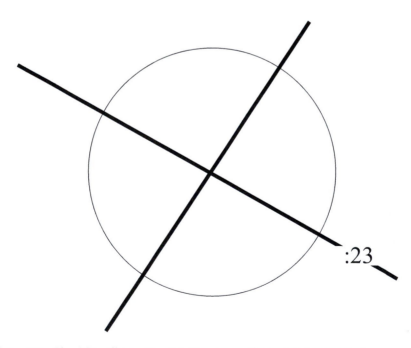

Figure 8.1c The AD will imagine this line across the watch face second

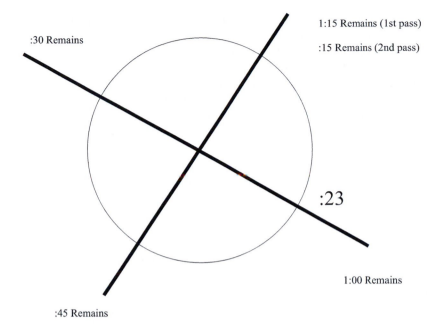

:30 Remains

1:15 Remains (1st pass)

:15 Remains (2nd pass)

:23

1:00 Remains

:45 Remains

Figure 8.1d Visual math

to SOT portions. The transition point between the VO portion and the SOT portion is mission critical for the production person assigned to Audio. It is at this point that the anchor's mic will be cut and the audio from a playback device brought in "full." The anchor must be completed with the prepared script (or skilled enough to ad lib into the bite) as well.

In order for the anchor to do this, the Floor Director will count them into the bite (the SOT portion) by relaying the count from the AD. Thus, it will go something similar to what follows: assume the example VO/SOT is 30 seconds long. The VO portion is :25 and the following SOT :05. When the Director calls for the video, the AD will begin the stopwatch.

When the watch shows :15, there are 10 seconds left to the bite. The AD will say, "count in 10, 9, 8, 7, 6, 5, 4, 3, 2, 1." The Floor Director will be relaying these commands to the anchor (using hand signals) as the anchor finishes the prepared script. The anchor must be finished (often they have to speed up) or their microphone may be "upcut" as the Audio operator cross-cuts to the audio source.

A common variation on the counting process is to count the anchor directly through IFB (switched talkback).

SOT/VO

Not only is the point of transition important between VO and SOT, the reverse is also true. When an SOT cuts to a VO, the Audio operator will need to open the anchor's microphone and "cut" the playback source audio – exactly as it ends. Although the process does not involve the Floor Director "counting" with the talent, the Floor will need to cue the talent to provide the VO for that portion of the tape.

A common variant that avoids the VO/SOT timing difficulty is only slightly smoother for the production crew. Separating the VO portion and the SOT portion onto separate clips (rolled from separate playback machines) can be a work-around. The SOT merely needs to be precisely rolled in such a way as to "hit" program as the anchor is finishing the VO portion.

While there is no danger of upcutting the anchor or missing any audio from the bite, the crew is running the risk of machine failure. The danger is that the SOT will not (or cannot) roll for some reason and the anchor is left to look foolish for introducing a bite that will not be viewed. However, if the producing staff avoids "previewing" the SOT in the VO scripting – avoids "we ran into Coach Auriemma after the game and here is what he had to say" – the VO will merely stand alone and not seem peculiar. The Director (and crew) can merely continue to the next story in the event of video failure. The advantages to separating the VO from the SOT really bear on the AD, the Floor Director, the anchor, and Audio. The disadvantages really affect the Director, the TD, and Playback. A zero sum game perhaps.

Character Generation

Another timing task that involves the video clip concerns the point at which character generation may be required to be keyed (layered) over the video clip. The AD may use the same stopwatch used for clip time for this task or may use an additional watch (digital or analog).

The point at which a particular graphic is to be brought up is usually very tight (often a window of no longer than 5 seconds). The graphic might be a location, "Portales, New Mexico," or a name, "David Vergobbi, Expert Witness." Names tend to be much more time critical as the person may only appear during a short soundbite.

The AD, then, will need to be ready to call the command to "key" in the graphic. Again, the timing of graphics is often delegated to another crew member (some Directors also act as their own ADs due to common "control" issues among the group). Yet, it is not uncommon for the TD or Graphics operator to handle the task. And, in with the widespread use of **non-linear editing (NLE)** systems, character generation is commonly pre-produced (edited) on the video clip prior to air.

NRCS control software, if so programmed, can access and activate graphic assets as associated with a video clip at predetermined marks on the clip. Thus, the entire graphics process can be somewhat automated.

DIRECTING

Introduction

The job of the Director is to "drive the bus." All of the other crew positions are coordinated by the command cues the Director gives as the show commences. To know "what to say and when to say it" the Director will primarily rely on the script, the rundown, and the critical timing information regarding any roll-ins (video clips).

The language the Director uses when giving these command cues is like a short-hand. It allows one person to communicate with the entire crew in an efficient manner. Learning the language is easy. Performing the language live is something else entirely.

No matter how well written the news program may be, no matter how skilled and experienced the producing staff and anchors, the show will fail if the Director cannot coordinate the production effort.

Director Wayne Nesbitt (the guy who trained your author) said, "Directing is like running in front of a train." "Either you are leading the train down the tracks, or you are being run over." In live television, there is no "time out" beyond that which is built into the show (commercial breaks).

The Command Cue Language

The command language is straightforward. A Director should give commands in a two-step flow: a "ready" cue that is followed by a "do it" cue. For example, a Director might say, "Ready Camera One" followed by "Take Camera One."

However, the process gains complexity as audio information is added. For example, a Director might say, "Ready Camera One with a Mic and a Cue" followed by "Take Camera One, Mic, and Cue."

Information can be added or deleted to the command syntax as necessary. For example, the Mic number can be added and the word "camera" deleted. "Ready One with Mic 4 and a Cue" followed by "Take One, Mic, and Cue."

A Director's particular style will determine the command syntax, but it is easy to see how giving the Mic number might get muddled with the Camera number in the mix of the headset chatter.

Another protocol you may already have noticed is to always follow the video cue with the audio cue. "Ready Camera Two with a Mic and Cue." Remember the basic form – a "ready" cue followed by a "do it" cue – it is the only way the crew can respond to direction calmly. Imagine a Director who never gives "ready" cues …

Command Cue Lexicon

Aside
Bust
Center-Up (Camera)
Clear
Come-Up (TD)
Crab (Camera)
Crash (Camera)
Cross-Fade (Audio)
Cue (Floor Director)
Cut (TD)
Dead
Dissolve (TD)
Dolly (Camera)
Downstream (TD)
Fade (Audio)
Fade (TD)
Fade to Black (TD and Audio)
Fade Up (TD)
Font (TD)
Full-Track (Audio)
Go (Audio)
Loosen (Camera)
Lose (TD)
Mic (Audio)
Mix (TD)
Pan (Camera)
Pedestal (Camera)
Pull (TD)
Push (TD)
Re-Rack (Tape)
Ready
Roll (Tape)
Roll Record (Tape)
Set-Focus (Camera)
Sneak (Audio)
Spin (Graphics)
Stand-By
Swing (Floor Director)
Take (TD)
Tighten (Camera)
Tilt (Camera)
Track (Audio)
Track (Camera)
Truck (Camera)
Wipe (TD)
Zoom

Figure 8.2 Command cue lexicon

CAMERAS VS. PLAYBACK MACHINES

In order to differentiate and separate camera commands from playback commands, the most common protocol in news is to number cameras and letter playback machines.

Savvy Directors will continue the separation in the command syntax by "readying" cameras and using "stand-by" for playback. For example, "stand-by DDR A" and "roll A … take it" is linguistically separate from "ready camera one" and "take one."

Add the audio information to the DDR command and the Director might say, "Stand-by DDR A, full-track is coming on A, roll A, track, and take it" or "Stand-by DDR B, NAT on Channel 2, roll B, take it, sneak NAT (or "Track the NAT")."

Remember, information can be added and deleted to the command syntax as necessary – and it is only really necessary to identify the playback machine once. For example, "Stand-by DDR A, full-track" followed by "Roll, track, take."

Other commands and many variations exist in the command cue lexicon. The command to activate a key might take any one of the following forms: "Stand-by downstream" followed by "Downstream" followed by "Ready to lose downstream" followed by "Lose." Or "Ready to font" followed by "Font" followed by "Ready to lose" followed by "Lose."

As a beginning Director, it is valuable to spend some time listening and watching "Director's Cuts" of newscasts. In a Director's Cut, the audio mix includes the headset/intercom chatter with the program video so that you can see (and hear) the connection between the command cue and the result.

MARKING SCRIPT

One of the procedures the Director will follow involves "marking" the script with reminders (memory jogs) as to what command needs to be said. Although, every Director marks script differently, a lowest common syntax is useful to learn the marking process.

"OC" stands-for On-Camera. A Director may jot OC1 to indicate that a particular segment is to be handled by camera one. OC2 would indicate that the primary video would be from camera two – and so on.

The mark for a pre-recorded clip is bit more complex. First, a **roll-cue** must be located and marked in the script. A roll-cue is a word that the anchor is to say in the few moments before a clip will be rolled and activated to program. Depending on the average speed of the anchor, the roll-cue could be an entire sentence or so "back" from the point of the clip hit.

Once the roll-cue is located and "marked" (some Director's will circle it), the DDR information will need to be marked into the script. One

Who Does What Part I

Figuring out the command cues can take time for the production crew. Consider how many people are involved by the following command, "Stand-By DDR A, Full-Track is coming on A, Roll A, Track, and Take."

On "Stand-By Tape A" the Playback operator has loaded the correct media and cued to the correct video clip in DDR A. The clip is cued (on pause) and the operator is poised to press play.

The TD has selected DDR A in the Preview Bus.

On "Full-Track is coming on A" the Audio operator prepares to cross-fade to the two audio channels that will be fed from DDR A.

On "Roll A" the Playback operator presses play.

On "Track" the Audio operator will crossfade to the DDR audio.

On "Take" the TD will transition to DDR A as the active program source.

Who Does What Part II

Or, consider the following command, "Ready Camera One with a Mic and a Cue, Take, Mic, and Cue."

On "Ready Camera One" the TD selects Camera One to the Preview Bus.

The Camera One Operator is poised with the appropriate shot.

The Floor Director is standing next to Camera One and is at Stand-By (arm up, palm out, fingers up).

On "Take" the TD transitions to Camera One as the active program source.

On "Mic" the Audio operator will "bring-up" the appropriate anchor microphone as the program audio source.

On "Cue" the Floor Director will cue the anchor in the studio to begin (swinging the arm downward). All of this illustrates that when a Director gives a command, many crew members can be responding almost at the same time.

Figure 8.3 Who does what?

technique is to make a roll box. In the example, notice the word "Roll" and the box below it. The word "roll" is a memory jog aimed at the roll command. The DDR letter can be marked in the box – in this example it is DDR A. Finally, an arrow can be drawn from the roll box toward the roll-cue in order to direct the eye.

Thus, while the anchor is reading the introductory portion of the story to camera one (as indicated by the OC1 mark), the Director can give the ready cue for DDR A. When the Director hears the anchor hit the roll-cue, the Director can "roll" the clip and "take" it as the program source as the anchor finishes the story introduction.

Other common marks include "**FTB**" or **Fade-to-Black**; "MC" for Master Control; "###" or "-30-" for the end of a segment (an old throw back – ask the oldest Journalism professor you can find).

140 – METEOR SHOWER

ANCHOR 1

OC1

OC1

STAR-GAZERS… GET READY. ASTRONOMERS SAY TONIGHT'S METEOR SHOWER MAY BE THE MOST IMPRESSIVE IN DECADES. RESIDENTS OF THE MIDWEST GOT AN EARLY VIEW OF THE LEONID METEOR SHOWER—AND MANY OF THEM CALLED AUTHORITIES TO REPORT U-F-OS. THE METEORS ARE DUST AND ICE PELLETS FROM THE COMET TEMPEL-TUTTLE. ASTRONOMERS SAY YOU COULD SEE AS MANY AS FIVE-THOUSAND PER HOUR. THEY SAY THE BEST TIME TO WATCH THE LEONID SHOWER IS IN THE EARLY MORNING HOURS. THE PEAK IS SUPPOSED TO BE JUST AFTER DARK… BUT LAST YEAR IN WILLIMANTIC… IT WAS OFF BY A FEW HOURS. SOURCES FROM LOWELL OBSERVATORY TELL US THAT THE BEST WAY TO SEE THE METEOR SHOWER IS JUST TO LOOK AT THE SKY… AND THE DARKER THE AREA YOU ARE IN… THE BETTER. ###

###

Figure 8.4 An example of a marked script page for a reader (OC)

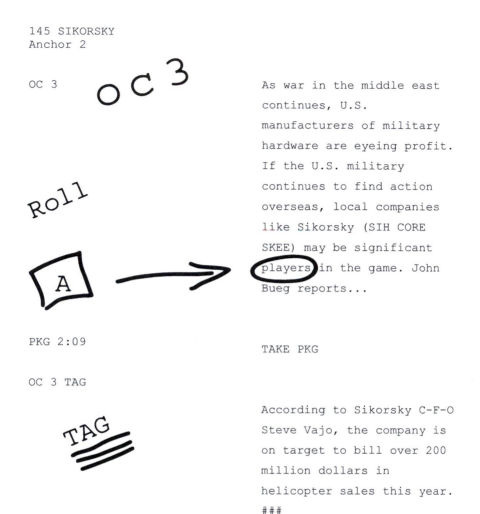

145 SIKORSKY
Anchor 2

OC 3

As war in the middle east continues, U.S. manufacturers of military hardware are eyeing profit. If the U.S. military continues to find action overseas, local companies like Sikorsky (SIH CORE SKEE) may be significant players in the game. John Bueg reports...

PKG 2:09

TAKE PKG

OC 3 TAG

According to Sikorsky C-F-O Steve Vajo, the company is on target to bill over 200 million dollars in helicopter sales this year.
###

Figure 8.5 An example of a marked script page for a package (PKG)

PRACTICE

It is important that new Directors do not attempt to write-out, verbatim, the command cues needed for a program on the script. The television program is in the monitors, not the script. If you are reading written commands, you are not directing. The more time you spend looking at the monitors, the fewer mistakes (out-of-focus cameras, wrong video clips, misspelled graphics) will make it to air. The script is only one tool in the procedure of directing and you must learn to merely glance at it as the show progresses. By all means one should practice command cues in whatever fashion seems to work well for the individual. However, it is good form to always direct from marks so that the new Director does not come to awkwardly rely on a script of command cues.

The time period immediately prior to the newscast is a busy one. Final preparations are made that concern both the producing staff and production crew. In the final minutes, Master Control will confirm communication with the Control Room as well as monitor the incoming flow of audio and video from any remote units. The crew member at Audio and the Technical Director will reconfirm all audio and video sourcing, and the synchronization of time clocks with Master Control. At the appointed time, Master Control will count the studio into the show by counting down the minutes and seconds and finish by activating the studio as the master source for the station – the studio is now "up." It is at this point that the program is in the hands of the production crew as the Director "calls" the show.

GLOSSARY

2D Animation: two-dimensional graphic that is programmed with movement.

3D Animation: three-dimensional graphic that is programmed with movement.

4K a line resolution protocol for UHDTV of 2160 horizontal lines. A "doubling" of the 1080 protocol.

8K A line resolution protocol for UHDTV of 4320 horizontal lines. A "doubling" of the 4K protocol.

16K A line resolution protocol for QUHDTV of 8640 horizontal lines. A "doubling" of the 8K protocol. QUHDTV is called Quad.

A1 (see Audio Operator).

A2 Audio Assistant.

AP Assistant or Associate Producer.

Affiliate (see Network Affiliate).

Air Check a master recording of a television show.

Anchors (see Talent).

Aside a command cue that temporarily suspends a segment from the rundown.

As-Live a procedure where the production of a television program is conducted as if the facility were live. A production carried out in "real time."

Aspect Ratio the ratio of width to height of the video image (typically 4:3 or 16:9). The shape of the image.

Assistant Director (AD) or Production Assistant (PA) production crew member responsible for timing a television program.

Audio Operator production crew member responsible for operating the audio board.

Audio Board   controls the selection, flow, modification and mix of audio sources. An audio selection device. The final output is Audio Program.

Audio Booth (also Audio Control)   a small room or area adjacent to the primary control room space where the audio board is located.

Audio Console   (see Audio Board).

Audio Monitor   a speaker in the control room used to monitor Audio Program.

Audio Program   the final mix of audio sent out for recording or broadcast.

Audio Snake   a cable containing bundled audio lines that terminates in a box containing multiple audio hook-ups.

Audio Source   any machine or device that generates an audio signal.

Aux Bus   a single row or a group of two rows of buttons on the video switcher that are selectively programmable.

Backlight   a lighting instrument located 45 degrees up and to the rear of a talent position. A backlight provides visual separation of the talent from the background.

Backfocus (or Flangeback)   the focus adjustment between the camera imaging device (CCD or CMOS) and the lens.

Bank Lighting   a lighting strategy that uses rows of flood lights to illuminate a set.

Barndoors   a four flap sheet metal lighting accessory mounted to the front of a lighting instrument that permits greater control in how a light is aimed.

Battens (or Barrels)   the lighting grid is made up of pipes called battens. Lighting instruments are mounted to battens.

Beltpack   a small box that is a component of the intercom system. The box connects the headset and audio cable, controls intercom channel selection, headset volume, and headset mic activation.

Biscuit   (see Tripod Shoe).

Block   a section of a television program that occurs between commercial breaks. A one-half hour news program is often broken into four blocks.

BNC   a type of professional grade, locking video connector.

Boundary Microphone (PZM)   a flat-shaped microphone designed to be mounted on flat surfaces (a stage, the middle of a table).

Broad   a non-focusing flood light shaped like a small box.

Broadcast Engineer   production crew member and station employee responsible for audio and video routing, signal quality, signal balance, and equipment repair.

Bug   a small graphic (usually a logo) keyed onto the Video Program signal at Master Control.

Bugged   any video containing a bug.

Bump   a transitional video clip that is played at the end of a program block just prior to commercial break. Often, the bump is used to tease content coming up later in the program.

Bust   a command cue to stop recording the television program.

Camera   (see Studio Television Camera).

Camera Cable   a cable that carries the video from the studio television camera to the control room.

Camera Control Units (CCUs)   a remote control for the studio television camera that is located in the control room. The CCU controls power, color balance, iris, and white and black balance.

Camera Operator   production crew member responsible for operating the studio television camera.

Camera Plate   a flat metal plate used in conjunction with a tripod shoe to attach a camera unit to a tripod or pedestal head.

Cardioid   (see Unidirectional).

Channel One   a channel of audio (the Left channel) sourced from a stereo audio source.

Channel Two   a channel of audio (the Right channel) sourced from a stereo audio source.

Character Generator (CG) or Caption Generator (CapGen)   a computer located in the control room that generates video text (words) that can be keyed over a picture or used alone as a video source. The CG function is commonly one capability of a central Graphics Computer.

Charged Metal Oxide Semiconductor (CMOS)   one type of imaging device inside the studio television camera. A CMOS (or chip) converts light into a video signal. Professional cameras have 3 chips, one to image red, one to image green, and one to image blue. The larger the CMOS, the higher the possible resolution.

Chroma Key Wall   a set piece that is painted a green or blue color (or a cyc or curtain that is dyed similar.) When viewed through the studio camera, the color can be isolated, removed, and replaced in the chroma key process. The weather forecast is usually delivered from the chroma key wall.

Chrominance   color saturation.

Clear   a command cue that indicates that audio from the playback devices and/or the microphones and/or the cameras are no longer active to program.

Clip   adjusts the relative strength of the video layer in the keying process. Clip adjustment is located on the video switcher.

Clip Store   a flash memory based area in a video switcher that can hold short, pre-recorded video clips.

Clip Time or Duration   the precise length of a video clip.

Color Bars   a video test pattern that contains colored bars.

Column Lock   a pedestal lock that prevents the camera from moving vertically.

Come Up   a command cue that instructs the TD to engage a dissolve (or fade) from Black to the video source in Preview.

Command Cue Language   the shorthand language that permits the Director to speak to and instruct the entire production crew at once.

Common Control Interface   a control surface on an audio board that, when activated, permits the modification of a specific input fader on an audio board.

Complementary metal-oxide semiconductor (CMOS)   one type of imaging device inside the studio television camera. A CMOS (or chip) converts light into a video signal. Professional cameras have 3 CMOS chips, one to image red, one to image green, and one to image blue.

Control Room   a physical space containing the staff and equipment that controls the flow and selection of audio and video in a television program.

Crossfade   a command cue for Audio to bring one audio source down while at the same time bringing another audio source up.

Cue   a command given by the Director to the production staff to begin a task or procedure. A command given to the talent to begin speaking. A video clip is cued when it is ready to be activated.

Cut   an instant transition between two video sources.

Cut Number   when multiple video clips are located on an individual piece of media, the cut number refers to the clip's identification, position or location.

Cut Sheet   (see Font Sheet).

Cyc light   a cyc light is a flood light designed to illuminate the cyc. Cyc lights will either be mounted on the ground and aimed up or grid mounted and aimed downward. Cyc lights are commonly colored using gels. Cyc lights are used to illuminate the chroma key wall (without gels).

Cyclorama (CYC)   a curtain or flat fabric panel that is available as a backdrop in the studio. Usually, cycs help to absorb echo and are non-reflective.

Dead   a story or technical segment has been permanently discarded from the rundown.

Decibel (dB)   a scale for measuring the strength of an audio signal. see also reference dBFS and dBu.

Digital Disk Recorder (DDR)   an audio/video playback and/or audio/video recording device. DDRs use removable flash memory media.

Digital Multi-Effects (DME)   (see Digital Video Effects).

Digital Multiplex (DMX)   a standardized network protocol that controls lighting instruments.

Digital Picture Manipulator (DPM)   (see Digital Video Effects).

Digital Video Effects (DVE)   a special effects processor either embedded within or hooked into the video switcher. A video source can be routed to the DVE, modified, and looped back to the switcher as a new source.

Direct Access Key   A button on a switcher that will activate a key layer to program instantly, thus bypassing the traditional "transition area" on the switcher.

Director   leader and supervisor of the production staff. Responsible for using the command cue language to "call" a television program.

Dissolve   a video transition where one video source is gradually replaced by another.

Dolly   (see Pedestal).

Dolly or Track   a command cue for the camera operator to roll the entire camera unit toward or away from the set.

Downstream Key (DSK)   a key that is electronically processed in the switcher after all transition and effects have been added to the Program Video.

Drag or Friction   (see Pan Friction or Tilt Friction)

Drive Number   an identifying number assigned to a specific computer drive (memory) device (hard drive, flash drive, etc.).

Duratran   a backlit, translucent image embedded in the flat wall of a set.

Edit Mode   an operating mode of a teleprompter that permits changes to the script to be made.

Electronic Memory (eMem)   A flash memory based storage device built into a video switcher. eMems save and recall switcher set-ups (or save and recall the "state" of the switcher).

Electronic Still-Store (ESS)   a graphics computer (or function of a graphics computer) that captures, stores, manages, sequences, and displays still-images. Many modern video switchers have embedded ESS capability (Grass Valley Image Store).

Ellipsoidal   a type of spot light used to create distinct shapes, patterns, and art on a set. An effects light.

Engineer   (see Broadcast Engineer).

Engineering   a physical place in a television station where equipment is repaired (called the bench); and, the location in the control room where the engineering equipment is located (CCUs, routing switchers, wave-form monitors, vectorscopes).

Equalization (EQ)   the process of increasing or decreasing the sensitivity of a specific audio frequency or group of frequencies.

Fade (audio related)   to slowly increase or decrease the strength of an audio source.

Fade (video related)   to engage a dissolve (mix) either up from Black to an active video source or down to Black (Fade-To-Black).

Faders   control the input and output flow of audio through the Audio Board.

Fader Bar   a T-shaped handle in the Transition Area on the video switcher that permits manual control of wipes and dissolves.

Feature   (see Package).

File Number   an identifying number assigned to a media file. A file "name."

Fill Light   the second light of the three-point lighting strategy. Located 45 degrees up and to the right of the talent position, the fill light may be a spot light or a flood light.

Filtering   a function of the audio board that permits the isolation of a specific frequency and the removal of all frequency response above or below that point.

Fixed Linear Key   (see Linear Key).

Flash Memory   non-volatile computer memory.

Flats   vertical set pieces used to create background walls for a set.

Flood Lights   lighting instruments that generate a type of light ray that is non-parallel and distanced apart. The quality of light is soft or diffused and the beam spread is wide.

Floor Director   production crew member responsible for managing and communicating with the talent. Floor Directors cue the talent, relay commands and timing information from the Control Room, assist other studio crew members, and are responsible for studio safety.

Focus   the property of visual clarity established between the camera lens and the targeted object.

Font Sheet or Clip Sheet   a document that contains information regarding a video clip (duration, audio characteristics, story type, graphics requirements).

Footcandle (FC)   a measure of light based on the amount of luminance given by a single candle at a distance of twelve inches.

Frame Memory   (see Freeze).

Framing   the composition of a camera shot refers to framing.

Freeze   refers to the capture of one frame of video to use in an ESS.

Fresnel   a focusing spot lighting instrument used for lighting people and set materials.

Friction or Drag   (see Pan Friction or Tilt Friction).

FTB   shorthand for Fade-To-Black.

FX   shorthand for effects (usually graphics or DVE).

Gaffers   production crew member responsible for hanging, aiming, and tuning the lighting instruments. Gaffers are often electricians.

Gain (audio related)   a control on the audio board that permits the amplification of an incoming signal.

Gain (key related)   a control on the video switcher that permits the amplification of the video source assigned to the key bus.

Gain (video related)   amplification of a video signal.

Gel   a colored sheet of non-flammable plastic used to color the light output of a lighting instrument.

Gobo   a logo or pattern cut from metal that can be inserted inside of an ellipsoidal light. The logo or pattern will project onto the surface the light is aimed toward.

Graphics   production crew member responsible for creating, managing, sequencing, and playing back character generation, still images, 3D models, and animations.

Graphics Computer   a computer designated for the creation of character generation, still images, 3D models, and animations.

Grips or Dolly Operators   production crew member responsible for assembling sets, managing boom mounted microphones, managing jib mounted cameras, and other manual tasks.

Ground Row   a lighting instrument that contains multiple in-line lamps used to wash light upward.

Handheld   the most common type of field microphone. Designed to be "held in the hand."

Hard Cyc   a chroma key colored cyclorama (CYC) made of hard material (typically in the shape of a skateboarding quarter-pipe (or one half of a clam-shell).

HDTV   high definition television any television signal that contains more than 480 lines of resolution. (720 lines of resolution or 1080 lines of resolution).

Headroom   the visual space between the top of the talent's head and the top of the image frame.

Headset   a component of the Intercom Unit worn on the head containing a headphone and a microphone.

HyperCardioid   a microphone pick-up or "polar" pattern that acquires sound in one direction with narrow and distance-extended characteristics.

Image Store   (see Electronic Still-Store).

Injest   the process of loading video into a video server.

Intercom Unit   the off-air communication system that includes the staff of the Control Room, the Studio, Master Control, and other production crew as needed.

Interrupt Foldback (IFB) or Switched Talkback   an audio feed of the entire program mix (excluding the anchor's own microphone) from the audio board to a small earphone worn by the talent on the set. IFB allows the talent to monitor Audio Program, and it also permits the producing staff to cut into the feed and speak directly to the anchor.

Input Fader   a sliding knob on the audio board that controls the input signal strength an individual audio source.

Instant Start   any type of playback device that permits the video clip to attain operating speed without pre-roll, countdown, or cue space.

ISO   isolation recording. A camera is said to be in "ISO" when the video feed from that camera is recorded apart from (and in addition to) video program.

Jackfield   (see Patch Panel).

Jib   a camera mounted to the end of a long, metal arm.

Key   a video layer.

Key Bus   a row of buttons on the video switcher that permits the selection and assignment of a key video source.

Key Light   the first light of the three-point lighting strategy. Located 45 degrees up and to the left of the talent position, the key light is usually a spot light.

Key Shot   a type of camera shot that includes an over-the-shoulder graphic. Also called a "box shot."

Key Source   a video source (such as the output of the graphics computer) that has been assigned to a key using the key bus.

Kicker   a light aimed at the background of a set from a left and/or right position off-screen.

Latch   a type of video transition where the background and a key are transitioned at the same time.

Lavalier   the most common type of studio microphone. Also known as a lapel mic, the unit is small and unobtrusive.

Lead-In   a short introductory sentence given on-camera by an anchor to introduce a video clip or live shot.

Leadroom or Looking Room   visual space given in the frame for the talent to walk into or look into.

Light Meter   a handheld meter that measures the intensity or amount of light.

Lighting Director (LD)   responsible for the overall design, installation, and appearance of the lighting in a studio or field production.

Lighting Board   a console that controls power flow to each lighting instrument. Permits dimming, grouping, and fading of the lighting instruments.

Lighting Grid   the large network of pipes and electrical service located in the ceiling of the studio.

Lighting Instrument   a generic term for any light used in the studio.

Line Source   an audio source that is generated at a normalized signal strength (DDRs, audio servers).

Linear Key   a type of key where the keyer in the video switcher cuts-out the basic shape of the key source and fills the screen with that image/graphic.

Live-feed   (see Live Shot).

Live Shot   a story format that features a reporter live on-the-scene. A live shot can be returned to the station via microwave, satellite, cellular telephone, or the internet.

Live to Tape   conducting a television program from beginning to end as if the program is a live broadcast. Also called As-Live.

Location (L)   the physical or virtual location of a pre-recorded video clip. Refers to a specific DDR, server channel, or computer file.

Locked   a command cue that indicates a video recording device is operating at speed and in the expected mode.

Loosen   a command cue for the television camera operator to zoom out.

Lose   a command cue for the Technical Director to deactivate a key.

Luminance   brightness.

Macro   a switcher oriented computer program that remembers a short sequence of button pushes.

Master Control or Transmission Control   a physical space in the television station where the output of the station is controlled from. Incoming microwave and satellite feeds are received and managed from Master Control. Commercial breaks, network feeds, pre-recorded programming, and live studio programming are controlled in this location.

Master Fader   a fader on the audio board that controls the signal strength of Audio Program.

Master Lock   a large, spring-loaded pin located through the pedestal head. A master lock prevents the camera from tilting.

Media Asset Management   the science, procedure, and protocol of managing video, audio, and graphics files on large, media object servers (MOS).

Media Object Server (MOS)   a central computer server that contains video, audio, and graphic "assets" that can be utilized (or accessed) by multiple devices across a network.

Mic Check   a pre-production task where the A1 checks and balances the incoming signal strength of a studio microphone.

Mic Source   audio generated from a microphone is weaker than audio generated by a Line Source by as much as 50 dB. Mic Sources need to amplified (see Gain) before mixing with Line Sources.

Microphone (MIC)   a transducer. A microphone changes sound waves to an electromagnetic signal.

Midstream Key   a key that is electronically processed in the switcher at the same time as the transition effects are added to Program Video.

Mix   (see Dissolve).

Mix Effects Bus (ME)   a group of three rows of buttons on a video switcher. An ME is made up of a Preview Bus (bottom row), a Program Bus (middle row), and a Key Bus (top row).

Mix Minus or Program Clean Feed (PCF)   audio program with the source audio from the anchor microphone removed. Permits the anchor to hear the show without danger of creating a feedback loop or distracting the anchor with a delayed feedback of their own audio.

Monitor   (see Video Monitor and/or Audio Monitor).

Monitor Wall   the monitor wall is the feature of the control room that contains numerous video monitors that reveal video sources that can be selected from, Preview Video and Program Video.

Mono   one unique, individual channel of audio.

Multi-Viewer   a large, overhead video monitor that is divided (using software) into multiple video viewing screens of varying size. The use of multi-viewers can replace the use of a Monitor Wall.

Mute   a switch located on an input fader on an audio board that silences an incoming audio signal regardless of the position of the fader knob.

Natural Sound (NAT) or Atmosphere (ATMOS)   audio from a video clip that is without reporter narration. Natural sound is "location" sound. i.e. birds chirping, wind noise, waves crashing, glass breaking, gunfire, or explosions.

Network Affiliate   a television station that is formally associated with a network. The relationship permits the local station to use the resources of the network (content, satellite time, etc.) and the network to "reach" a large audience.

News Desk   a prominent feature of the news set where the anchors sit and deliver the newscast.

News Director   the ultimate producer responsible for a television news operation.

Newsroom Computer System (NCS or NRCS)   top level "organizing" software that manages the rundown, the script, and the media assets for a news program.

Non-Linear Editing (NLE)   computer based, non-chronological editing.

NTSC   National Television Standards Council (see SDTV).

Omnidirectional   a microphone pick-up or "polar" pattern that acquires sound in all directions.

On-Camera (OC)   a story format where the anchor merely reads a story to a camera with no associated pre-recorded video clip.

Outcue (see also Standard Outcue)   the last thing seen and/or heard on a pre-recorded video clip.

Overmodulation   an audio signal that is too strong. The excess electrical strength will distort the signal.

Over the Shoulder (OTS)   a camera shot of one person from a position behind a second person – revealing the back of the head and shoulders of the second person.

Output Fader   a sliding knob or set of knobs on the audio board that controls the output signal strength of Audio Program.

Package (PKG)   a story format that features an on-camera introduction by the news anchor followed by a pre-recorded video clip.

PAD   extra material edited to or remaining on the tail of a video clip.

Pan   a command cue for the camera operator to pivot the camera to the left or to the right.

Pan (audio)   a knob located on an input fader of an audio board that will "send" the output of that fader to either the right channel of audio program or the left channel of audio program.

Pan Friction or Drag   an adjustment on the pedestal head that will provide "resistance" to the right/left pivoting control of the camera.

Pan Lock   a pedestal lock that prevents the camera from pivoting left and right.

PAR   Parabolic Aluminum Reflector light, a type of lighting instrument with a fixed beam spread.

Panel   a type of LED flood light (box shaped).

Patch Panel   an input/output box of audio, video, intercom, and clock connections located on a studio wall.

Pedestal   the mount for the studio television camera.

Pedestal   a command cue for the camera operator to raise or lower the height of the camera.

Pedestal Steering Wheel   a wheel that is located mid-level on a studio camera pedestal that is used for pushing, pulling, and steering a studio television camera.

Percent of Modulation (PM)   a measurement scale of audio signal strength on a 0 to 100 scale.

Phantom Power   a feature of some audio boards that sends a 48 volt channel of Direct Current (DC) upstream in order to power a studio microphone.

Pickup Pattern   (see Polar Pattern).

Playback   production crew member responsible for the management and playback of video clips in a television program. Playback is often responsible for recording the program as well.

Polar Pattern   the acquisition or directional characteristic (or pickup shape) of a microphone.

Post-Fade   an audio signal after modulation by the audio board fader strip.

Post-Production   the process of or facility for video editing.

Pre-Fade   an audio signal prior to modulation by the audio board fader strip.

Pre-Set (PST)   (see Preview).

Pressure Zone Microphone (PZM)   see Boundary Microphone.

Preview (PVW)   the video source that is on-deck, or next-in-line.

Preview Bus   a row of buttons on the video switcher that permits the direct selection of the Preview Video source.

Producer   the writer or a member of the writing staff.

Program (PGM)   the final mix of audio and/or video sources that is assembled as a television program.

Program Bus   a row of buttons on the video switcher that permits the direct selection of the Program Video source.

Prompt Mode   an operating mode of a teleprompter where a script is actively in "recall" and "viewable" by the talent.

QUAD   (see 16K).

Reader   (see On-Camera).

Ready (see also Standby)   a command cue to prepare for a task that follows.

Remote (REM)   a story format that features a live-feed from remote location.

Resolution   the number of horizontal lines of video information that, when viewed together on a video monitor, create an image. For example, one resolution protocol for HDTV is expressed as 1080. The image is made up of 1080 lines.

Return Video   a feature on the camera (typically located as a button on the servo-zoom control) that, when activated, will allow the camera operator to see various (as routed) video sources in the camera view-finder (typically program).

Risers   platforms used in set construction to raise the actual and visual height of a set.

Roll   a command cue for Playback to play a pre-recorded video clip.

Roll-Cue   a specific word in the script identified by the Director as the cue to convey a Roll command. Usually a roll cue is selected a few seconds prior to the expected take point of the clip.

Roll Record   a command cue for Playback to engage a video recording device to record Video/Audio Program.

Routing Switcher   a device that directs incoming audio and/or video signals to specific destinations. Also called a "router."

Run Number   an identifying number assigned to a specific, individual segment in a television program.

Rundown   an outline of a television program that lists the segments of the program.

Scan Protocol   the manner in which one frame of video (one image) changes to the next frame of video. Scan protocols are expressed as "i" for interlace scan and "p" for progressive scan.

Scene Dock   a room (often adjacent to the studio) used for the storage of set materials.

Scoop   an older type of flood light shaped like a large mixing bowl.

SDTV (see NTSC)   standard definition television: any television signal made up of 525 lines of resolution (analog) or 480 lines of resolution (digital) at 30 frames per second (black and white) and 29.97 frames per second (color).

Segment Number   (see Run Number).

Select   a feature on an audio console that activates or "chooses" an input fader for manipulation by the common control interface.

Set Designer   responsible for the overall design, construction, and appearance of a set.

Set Focus   a command cue instructing the camera operator to zoom-in as far as possible to the target subject followed by the careful adjustment of the focus control.

Shader   a member of the production staff responsible for "riding" the iris on the cameras during a live production.

Shotgun Microphone   a type of microphone constructed in a long, cylinder shape.

Shot Sheet   a list of camera shots that includes framing and composition information.

Show Time   the running total of the duration of a television program.

Signal Strength   a measure of electrical strength of a video or audio signal.

Sky Cyc   a flood light mounted in the grid (often a softbox) that is purposed to wash the CYC with light from the top downward.

Slug or Item   a short nickname given to a segment of a television program.

Snake   (see Audio Snake)

Sneak   a command cue to slowly fade-in an audio source.

Softlight (Softbox)   a box shaped floodlight.

Solo   a switch on the audio board that permits the operator to isolate and monitor a single audio source apart from the mix.

Sound-on-Tape (SOT)   indicates that source audio is contained on both channels of a video clip.

Spill   unwanted light. Light that has "spilled" over the intended target.

Spin   a command cue for graphics to activate a sequence of graphics pages or animation.

Spot Lights   lighting instruments that generate a type of light ray that is parallel and close together. The quality of light is hard and the beam spread is tight.

Stand-by (see also Ready)   a command cue to prepare for a task that follows.

Standard Outcue   refers to the standard manner of ending a pre-recorded video clip (typically a PKG or a REM) by a reporter. Usually, this is the name of the reporter followed by the name of the news organization. "I'm Todd Hicks ... Palo Alto News 9."

Stand Microphone   a type of microphone designed to "stand" by itself on a table top or other surface; or, a type of microphone designed for audio control booth applications. Similar to the handheld.

Stereo   two unique, individual, separate channels of audio.

Still-Store   (see Electronic Still-Store).

Studio   the large space in a television station where the set for a television program is located. The studio contains lighting equipment, audio acquisition equipment, and the studio television cameras.

Studio Camera Operator   the production technician assigned to operate the studio television camera.

Studio Television Camera   a device that creates a video signal from reflected light.

SuperCardioid   a microphone pick-up or "polar" pattern that acquires sound in one direction with narrow and distance-extended characteristics.

Swing   a command cue to motion the talent from one camera to another.

T-Bar   (see Fader Bar).

Tag   when the anchor will provide an on camera closing comment following a pre-recorded segment.

Take   a command cue to "cut" the video source in Preview to Program.

Talent   generic term for the individuals who host television programs.

Tally Light   located on the viewfinder, the tally light indicates whether the camera is "active" or selected to the program bus.

Tape   (see Playback).

Technical Director (TD)   production crew member responsible for operating the video switcher.

Teleprompter   production crew member responsible for the management, recall, and display of the prompting script.

Teleprompting Computer   a computer located in the control room that contains the script for the television program. The teleprompting software converts the script from text to video and allows the controller to "scroll" through the script.

Three-Point Lighting   a lighting strategy that uses three lighting instruments per talent position. The lights are the key light, the fill light, and the back light.

Tight Out   a video clip that ends immediately after the outcue. A video clip with no pad.

Tighten   a command cue for the camera to zoom in, tightening the framing.

Tilt   a command cue for the studio camera operator to either pivot the camera upward or downward.

Tilt Friction or Drag   an adjustment on the pedestal head that will provide "resistance" to the up/down pivoting control with the camera.

Tilt Lock   a pedestal lock that prevents the camera from tilting up or tilting down.

Tone   a 1 kHZ audio signal used to calibrate the audio board and the audio input of the recording devices.

Total Running Time (TRT)   refers to the complete duration of a television program or video clip.

Tough Spun   diffusion material affixed to the front of a lighting instrument that will soften the character of the light and reduce the overall output of that light (as measured with a light meter).

Track   a command cue for audio to fade-in the audio source from a video clip.

Transition   the manner in which one video source replaces another. The three common transitions on the video switcher are the cut, the wipe, and the dissolve.

Translite   (see Duratran).

Triple Key   a lighting strategy that uses three forward lights to illuminate a subject (45 degrees left, 90 degrees head-on, and 45 degrees right). Combined with a backlight, triple key is a slight modification of the three-point lighting strategy.

Trim   (see Gain audio related).

Tripod Shoe   a small plate that is used to attach the camera plate to the tripod.

Truck or Crab   a command cue for the studio camera operator to roll the entire camera left or to the right.

UHDTV   Ultra-High Definition Television. A television signal made up of more than 1080 lines of resolution (see 4K and 8K and 16K "quad").

UltraCardioid   a microphone pick-up or "polar" pattern that acquires sound in one direction with extremely narrow and distance-extended characteristics.

Undermodulation   an audio signal of little electrical strength.

Unidirectional   a microphone pick-up or "polar" pattern that acquires sound in one direction.

Vectorscope   a machine used by the Engineer to monitor chrominance (color) levels.

Video Background (BKGD)   the primary or dominant video source as used in Preview and Program.

Video Clip Time   the precise duration of a video clip.

Video File Format   the specific file encoding protocol for a digital video file. Expressed as the file extension (.mp4, .mov, .avi).

Video File Server   a PC and server-based video storage and playback system.

Video Monitor   a video monitor is a video viewing device.

Video Operator   (see Shader).

Video Playback Device   any machine that can play a pre-recorded video clip. Playback devices can also record a video/audio signal.

Video Program   the final mix of video sources flowing from the video switcher.

Video Switcher or Vision Mixer   a video selection console operated by the Technical Director.

Video Tape Recorder (VTR)   an analog or digital audio/video playback and recording tape machine (a legacy item).

Viewfinder   a small video monitor located on the top of the studio television camera that shows the operator what the camera is seeing.

Virtual Set   A set generated by computer software where the camera image is keyed over the output of that graphics computer. See also Chroma key.

Voice-Over (VO)   a story format that features the anchor narrating over video.

Voice-Over followed by Sound On Tape (VO/SOT)   a story format that begins with the anchor narrating over video (VO) immediately followed by an audio cut to a pre-edited sound bite sourced from the tape (SOT).

Volume   a human perception of loudness.

Volume Unit (VU)   a measurement scale of audio signal strength.

Waveform Monitor   a machine used by the Engineer to monitor video luminance (black and white) or "brightness" levels.

Wheel Lock   a lock located on the pedestal dolly wheel that prevents the wheel from rotating.

White-balance   a procedure that is used to calibrate the manner in which a camera references color. The value of white in a given lighting environment.

Wipe   a video transition that uses an effect to separate the outgoing video source from the incoming video source.

X-Axis   horizontal axis.

XLR Cable   a three-wire audio cable (three pin).

Y-Axis   vertical axis.

Z-Axis   depth axis.

Zoom   a command cue for the studio camera operator to engage the servo-zoom controller (either to zoom "in" or to zoom "out").

INDEX

Page numbers in *italics* refer to figures.

195

9780367199227